*Businesses are changing quickl[...]
why a fresh perspective of lead[...]
businesses is very welcome. W[...]
our values and behaviours from
a modern and futuristic perspective.
Based on practical and new research examples, the book
provides a comprehensive and serious rule book of
proven success stories that I fully
endorse from my forty years of experience.
Everyone will have a favourite section. The book is an
easy read, so that all leaders can use it as a valuable
reference. I'm hoping it will help you be MAD ("Make A
Difference") in your business!*
**Dame Mary Perkins, Founder &
Doug Perkins, Chairman and Founder Specsavers**

*The Leaders Book is music to my ears. It has some of the
best lessons in leadership that I've ever seen — covering
moral courage, high conviction leadership, legacy-
minded leadership (i.e. thinking beyond the horizon), a
character serving other people, implementing principles
with compassion and always doing the right thing as an
authentic leader that generates trust. It's a must read for
anyone who wants to be a better leader.*
**Lord Bilimoria of Chelsea CBE DL
Vice President (former President) of CBI (Confederation
of British Industry); Founder and Chairman, Cobra Beer;
Chancellor, University of Birmingham; Director,
International Chambers of Commerce (ICC) UK**

Leadership decisions impact lives and create a legacy which outlasts that leader. But what are the right decisions? What are the pitfalls in that leadership journey? Will the future have the footprint of our leadership today? All this is explored in this excellent book packed with leadership stories and case studies written by leaders for leaders.

Paul Hudson
National Regional Leader & Global Secretary for the Elim Pentecostal Movement

This is a leadership book rooted in the reality of leading in complex situations with practical, applicable examples. It's refreshingly focused on values first; using a moral compass to shape leadership styles. I recommend this to old and new leaders alike across all leadership contexts.

Keren Pybus
CEO & Co-founder Ethical Apparel Africa

Leadership is a human endeavour and this insightful and thought-provoking book gets to the heart of why this is so. It aims to explore the enduring fundamentals of moral courage, trust and a purpose beyond self. Supported by founding principles such as values, integrity, character and service, it lays bare the essence of a much-heralded but too often misunderstood concept. It's a book that dives deep into the core components of leadership, unravelling its complexity with ease and proving both highly accessible yet constructively challenging. Matching these core principles with "thought, word and deed," you will undoubtedly be a more effective leader.

Langley Sharp MBE
Founder & Director Frontier Leadership

This is an engaging book, crammed full of reminders on some key facets of leadership: courage, trust and legacy. I particularly like the section on "Temptations" – so very real! A great read for every leader and a guarantee of a couple of nuggets to take into your day job in each chapter.

Gill Palfrey-Hill
Director at Costa Coffee

The Leaders Book

Phil Eyre
Kareena Hodgson
Nicole Le Goupillot

Copyright © 2023 Phil Eyre, Kareena Hodgson, Nicole Le Goupillot

The moral right of the authors have been asserted.

Apart from any fair dealing for the purposes of research or private study, or criticism or review, as permitted under Copyright, Design and Patents Act 1998, this publication may only be reproduced, stored or transmitted, in any form or by any means, with prior permission in writing of the publishers, or in any case of the reprographic reproduction in accordance with the terms of licences issued by the Copyright Licensing Agency. Enquiries concerning reproduction outside these terms should be sent to the publishers.

PublishU Ltd

www.PublishU.com

All rights of this publication are reserved.

Thanks

We're grateful for the very many people and experiences that have contributed to our thoughts and this book. We'd like to thank again Sarah Gillard, Matt Bird and Major General Patrick Marriott for their encouragement and support.

We also want to acknowledge Dr Charles (Chuck) Coker, founder of LifeThrive Inc. Chuck is a wonderful source of encouragement and generosity, a great friend, talented thought leader and an exemplar of humility. Chuck's life and work are both inspiring and illuminating.

Contents

Introduction   "Leaders" founder Phil Eyre

Moral Courage

Foreword   Major General Patrick Marriott CB, CBE, DL

Morally Courageous Leaders ...

Chapter 1   Decide with High Conviction
Chapter 2   Implement with Compassion
Chapter 3   Resist Immediate Gratification
Chapter 4   Do the Right Thing
Chapter 5   Embrace the Defining Moments

Authentic Trust

Foreword   Matt Bird, Business and Social Entrepreneur

Trustworthy Leaders ...

Chapter 6   Do Not Hide
Chapter 7   Relate Well
Chapter 8   Walk the Walk
Chapter 9   Exercise Good Judgement
Chapter 10   Share Power

Living Legacy

Foreword   Sarah Gillard, CEO of A Blueprint for a Better Business

Legacy-Minded Leaders ...

Chapter 11   Prioritise Purpose

Chapter 12   Think Beyond the Horizon

Chapter 13   Make Leaders not just Followers

Chapter 14   Consider Whole-Community Impact

Chapter 15   Spread the Joy!

Concluding Thoughts Phil Eyre

Notes

About the Authors

THE LEADERS BOOK

THE LEADERS BOOK

Introduction

Every workplace in the world is a place where people flourish. That's our vision for the future. A far-off future perhaps, but one that compels us and shapes everything we do. Workplaces can and must be platforms that enable people to be the best of what it means to be human — creative, relational and resourceful creatures. Whether a workplace becomes so is substantially down to the influence and quality of its leaders. Leaders not only set direction for their organisations, but also curate the environment. Their attitudes, actions and choices will have the strongest bearing on whether their companies are healthy and flourishing, toxic and suffocating or somewhere in-between.

We've therefore dedicated ourselves to encouraging excellent leadership. It's by far the most effective way that we can play a part in making a positive difference, a step towards a world of flourishing workplaces. By encouraging, challenging, listening and speaking with leaders, we will contribute in our own small way to making work better for many thousands of people that we'll never meet.

This book is part of that intention. We're grateful to you for reading it. We deeply hope that it helps to strengthen your leadership. Even if just one idea of the many we are sharing resonates with you, for us, that's a job well done!

Our proposition is that excellent leaders carry three enduring qualities — they're morally courageous, trustworthy and lead with a living legacy mindset. Our work in these areas is informed by a plethora of influences and experiences. The following three stand out:

Major General Patrick Marriott (retired) CB, CBE, DL, Lord Lieutenant of Sutherland, and former Commandant of the Royal Military Academy Sandhurst, is exceptional — not only in his extensive career and service to his country, but in character. He brims with humility, generosity and integrity. He's a superb communicator; touching hearts and minds with alacrity. Patrick introduced us to "The Centre for Army Leadership," including their inaugural conference, titled "The Role of Leaders in Building a Culture of Moral Courage." It was there that we discovered the depth in the concept and honed what defines a morally courageous leader. I won't forget the profoundly moving talk on moral dilemmas given there by the Right Honourable Jack Straw. We're grateful to Patrick for his wisdom, ongoing support and contribution to this book.

We first encountered Matt Bird in 2014, shortly after his book ("Relationology: 101 Secrets to Growing Your business Through the Power of Relationships") was published. He's a serial entrepreneur; passionate about making a real-world impact in communities, business and government. He inspires us to stretch our limits, think bigger and foster deeper relationships. Matt introduces the section of this book on authentic trust.

Once in a while, we meet someone who we immediately and instinctively know exemplifies everything that we stand for. They simply have "it." Sarah Gillard, CEO of "A Blueprint for A Better Business," is one such person. She's made and continues to make a lasting impact on us.

She's the most living legacy-minded person that we know and there's no better person to introduce this section of our book to you.

We've written this book in the way that we lead ourselves. It's teamwork: three authors sharing team ideas in our individual, unique style. We've not attributed particular authors to chapters. You'll likely prefer one style over the other. We encourage you to not let that put you off the styles you find less easy. We've chosen not to include pages of exercises throughout, nor quote extensively from research. This is a distillation of our core proposition as to what makes for excellent leadership rather than a course workbook. We believe that you'll reflect on and apply the ideas that jump out to your specific situation — that's what good leaders do.

We're grateful for good leaders. Your commitment to growing your leadership (you wouldn't be reading this book otherwise) is a sign that you're already doing a good job. We're grateful for you. The world needs you.

Phil Eyre,

Founder, Leaders

THE LEADERS BOOK

Moral Courage

THE LEADERS BOOK

Foreword
Morally Courageous Leaders
Major General Patrick Marriott CB, CBE, DL

We all admire courage. It matters not whether it's shown by friend or foe — courage is always respected. C.S. Lewis would contend that it's the greatest of the virtues: "Courage isn't simply one of the virtues but the form of every virtue at the testing point, which means at the point of highest reality." Without courage, no real decision or act can be made in adversity.

Moral courage is the mental power to overcome wrongdoing, to act rightly, to do the right thing when the tide is against you or even just when no one's looking. Physical courage is the inner power to master the fear of bodily hurt. Moral courage can often engender physical courage. Men and women of principle are often very brave indeed.

Without moral courage so many (if not all) other virtues fail. Fairness can be lost; it takes moral courage to "speak truth to power." Wisdom can falter, right decisions against peer pressure are never easy; restraint or self-control is never simple when provocation endures.

Courage is thus one of the building blocks for good leadership. Without courage good behaviours frequently depart. Trust is eroded and leaders must be trusted and can only be trusted if they have integrity. And integrity often demands courage. It's easy to think rightly, but it's more difficult sometimes to speak rightly and very often much more difficult to do rightly. Integrity is when thought, word and deed openly align.

But, like leadership, courage can be developed. Soldiers are emboldened by good training and education: confidence is built and limits are exceeded. Gradually what seemed terrifying can seem quite benign. A first swim in cold water for anyone can be quite a challenge but once accomplished, the second becomes easier. Moral courage can be fortified by small right steps or golden rules: "Do as you'd be done by" or "Do as you ought, not as you want," such as exercises to practise public speaking or through group discussions.

But surely, some would say, bad leaders can find courage through self-interest and greed. That's true, but they're less easily followed and such motivations sow discords. Self-interest wavers constantly and is, by definition, not based on the team. Envy surely follows and from such cracks great fissures surely come. I'm afraid the only conclusion is that truly great leadership requires selflessness of the highest order. Leaders "serve to lead." That preparedness to serve others at the expense of oneself is perhaps one of the litmus tests by which others judge leaders — and quite rightly.

This short section of the book will examine much of this. If nothing else, let it teach its readers that first step of moral courage, to "think through others' eyes." That little glimpse of selflessness will, at the least, start to set the moral compass right. It'll start the process of knowing what must be done. The knowledge that a decision is right will stir the conscience to make it so.

THE LEADERS BOOK

Courageous leaders are willing to sacrifice their own comfort, their advancement, their rewards and recognition in the service of others.

Chapter 1
Morally Courageous Leaders
Decide with High Conviction

Morally courageous leaders make decisions based off of a deep conviction. All their decisions are made with an informed certainty. This is neither blind faith nor thoughtless instinct: it's grounding decisions in good character, experience and an acute respect for healthy personal values. For leadership excellence, making a quality decision is better than speed or quantity every time.

Yet it's common, easy in fact, for us to allow negative and undermining ideas to influence our choices, especially when presented with a dilemma (a choice that will negatively impact someone or everyone in one way or another). We can procrastinate and put off the important decision, comforting ourselves by focussing instead on lesser issues. We can allow other people's opinions, sometimes their threats, to cause us to flip-flop. We can make reactive choices — instantly jumping to conclusions before considering the implications.

The underlying reason for these and other unhelpful approaches to tough choices is fear. Fear is a natural and powerful emotion. This is understandable and — in measured ways — essential. When our fear takes too strong a hold on our choices, we set ourselves up for a lower-quality decision; sometimes even a destructive one.

What's needed is courage. Moral courage. To do the right thing. Courage requires conviction — a confidence in the decision. Conviction combined with compassion (the subject of the next chapter), propels us to do the right thing.

True leaders not only encounter dilemmas, but they also frequently initiate them, recognising that courageous choices are essential in order to achieve a better future.

Clarity

Leaders with deep conviction are clear about two critical things: firstly, the purpose of the organisation. In fact, they're possessed by what makes their particular organisation unique and useful to the world. They know what human or environmental problem their company is attempting to solve and the opportunity for others that their organisation is seeking to create. They believe genuinely that their organisation is improving the lives of other people and/or the natural environment. It's more than a job or task to be completed. Purpose carries meaning, making a positive difference to the world in some way (even if only in a small corner of it).

Second, they have a clear vision for the future of their company. Having a lofty idea about purpose and meaning is the beginning of high levels of motivation. Defining what the company's future impact could look like in practice ensures that motivation (or "movement") is focused and therefore effective. This blend is powerful, essential even, in setting the conditions for mobilising people, allocating resources and making choices with deep conviction.

Clarity of purpose and vision avoids the mission-creep trap. Creative ideas are an important part of good leadership. The trap is sprung when leaders forget about the purpose of their organisation and pursue ideas that detract from it. Acquiring an undervalued business might add to the bottom line, but if that business is at odds with the underlying purpose of your company, eventually value will be destroyed. Ditto new products, services and ways of operating.

CVS Healthcare provides us with an illustration. CVS is one of the largest retail pharmacies in the USA, committed to improving people's health and with a purpose statement that they're in fact bringing their heart to every moment of our health. Until 2014, this included selling cigarettes — one of the major causes of poor health. It became clear to CVS that this was at odds with their purpose, prompting them to cease tobacco sales, with an estimated loss in revenues of 2 billion USD. Whilst there are additional reasons for this decision (and other ways that the company raised its revenues), clarity of purpose was at the core.

Effective leaders will invite other people's perspectives to help inform and shape both purpose and vision. We are wary of leaders who are sole bearers of purpose and vision; it should be "ours" and not "mine." Including other people's experiences provides for a stronger vision and accountability: no single leader has a monopoly on good ideas. The finesse is that good leaders are not over-informed. They listen to other people, but not so many as to confuse their thinking, cloud their choices and chop-

and-change their decisions. They most certainly don't allow other people to substantially change purpose or vision — at least not without extensive consideration.

These are priority challenges for all leaders:

- How clear are we about the purpose of our organisations and how are we making the world a better place?
- How would anyone else know and what is the evidence in support of our purpose?
- Are we blind to compromises, like a healthcare company selling cigarettes?
- Are we clear about the actual beneficial impact we intend to make and our vision for the future?
- Are we focusing our efforts, resources and people towards this vision?
- Are we becoming distracted from what makes us unique and valuable?

Clarity about where our organisation is heading (vision) and why we're leading it there (purpose) is essential to making high-quality decisions.

Character

If you've worked with someone who achieves outcomes but is a tyrant, you'll know precisely why good character is important for leadership excellence. Who wants to follow someone of weak character?

Character informs the quality of our decisions; how courageous we're willing to be. "Goodness" (however defined) is the key characteristic that differentiates between courage and bravado. Courage is considered action, even if only for a moment. Bravado utterly ignores the risks to self and others: it is reckless.

The best leaders pursue courage, not recklessness, forging a sound character. They recognise that the quality of how a decision is made and implemented is just as important (often more important) than the decision itself. According to Dr Matthew Anderson, Executive Fellow of the University of Aberdeen, there are consistent ideas globally as to what constitutes morality and to doing the right thing. They're to be "of good character and ethically virtuous, upholding truth and justice, through kindness, honour, integrity, magnanimity and defending the weak and powerless." These may sound like lofty ideals and yet we'd all do well to consider these qualities when assessing whether we're making a "good" decision. The best leaders certainly do.

Personal values therefore play an important part in making high conviction decisions. Being clear about the kind of person that we want to be and become — not just the outcomes we want to achieve — sets the direction for our choices. For example, if we want to be known as someone who "upholds truth," then that will propel us to speak up when we should, provide fair reports of the situations that we're in and an honest assessment of the prospects for the future. If instead we're driven by career recognition or financial success, we'll likely make different decisions in the same scenarios — with no lesser conviction.

It's important to stress here that high conviction choices are based on a leader's personal values. These aren't quite the same (indeed sometimes entirely different) as corporate values. Corporate values have their place in guiding company direction and informing culture. But it's the power of deeply held, high conviction values that truly moves us to action. Understanding what truly matters to us and living out those priorities in practice is fundamental to being authentic — neither faking it nor ducking out of our responsibilities.

Morally courageous leaders can navigate through conflicts in values: firstly, their own inner conflicts. For most people, there's tension between our personal values. For example, "upholding truth" isn't always compatible with "joy." Excellent leaders understand which of their own values matter the most and should take priority in each situation. They also understand and respect other people's values and are able to identify which should take precedence. This will sometimes involve placing their own personal priorities in submission to someone else's. Such a leader won't view this as a compromise but as confidence that they're making the best decision.

Are you certain about your values, the character qualities or motivators that take precedence in any scenario — home, work and play? It would be worth taking a few moments, even now as you read this, to affirm to yourself the qualities that you truly care about: the person you want to be deep down. How closely connected are your values with Dr Anderson's summary of morality, noted a few moments ago? How willing are you to set aside your priorities when needed in order to make a better decision?

Others-Minded

True courage places other people as a priority rather than self; serving other people takes precedence. Bravado is self-centred. Such leaders are egoistical and destructive.

Courageous leaders are willing to sacrifice their own comfort, their advancement, their rewards and recognition in the service of others: especially the people in their teams and organisations. They aren't obsessed by their own careers and position. Instead, they're determined to support and challenge their people to grow and develop. They get excited when an up-and-coming high performer accelerates and overtakes them; whether that's a promotion within their own organisation or to a position elsewhere.

Our self-preservation and self-centred instincts are strong. It takes character and consistent effort to keep other people as a priority. It's surprisingly easy to blame others for mistakes and take credit for all successes; to disguise our own errors whilst highlighting other people's mistakes. It's easy to impose policies on others and excuse ourselves from following them and to make choices that inflate our own share options without considering those who will follow. Performative service (doing something for others as a means of self-promotion) has become an industry in itself: donating to charity, cleaning the environment, appointing minorities to boards with the intent of impressing other people, rather than simply because it's the right thing.

We're not against promotional activity, including talking about good social and ethical actions. But it's the primary intent that matters. If you aim to inspire others to similar action — great! If you seek to inflate your own sense of self-satisfaction — not so great.

Courageous leaders are empathetic in that they choose to think of the situation from other people's perspectives. How will they see this? What might they be feeling about it? Great leaders are keenly aware of their own emotions and how these are likely to impact others. They apply their own emotions in the service of others. Rather than tell everyone else how they're feeling, excellent leaders seek to understand what others are experiencing. They don't assume that everyone's feeling the same way as they are. Weak leaders are immersed in their own feelings and emotions: like the CEO who told me he felt upset at the difficult decision to lay off some of his staff. I asked how he thought they felt — he hadn't even considered them.

Being others-minded also includes thinking of people who aren't there yet: future employees, clients, suppliers and other stakeholders. Rather than extract as much personal gain as possible from the organisation (financial gain, reputable gain and future opportunities), courageous leaders think first about those who will follow. They want to leave their organisations in better shape than when they arrived and — here's the true test — they genuinely wish their successor even greater success. They take no pleasure at all in their successors' failures.

Sometimes, in order to understand how other people feel, we need to experience the situation personally. Leaders who are remote from the coalface might believe that they are making strong, objective decisions, but they're missing a critical, possibly the most critical, element; how other people are experiencing the situation. If there's a crisis in our companies, we need to visit it and experience it as best we can. Speak with the people actually involved directly. Relying solely on third party reports is risky. Being confronted personally with the problem can be unnerving but that's where true courage and therefore the strongest decisions are forged.

Developing an others-minded attitude takes consistent practice. Frequently asking ourselves questions like these, even better inviting trusted friends and colleagues to ask us, will help us to develop our serve-to-lead convictions:

- On whom am I directing the spotlight of praise?
- Am I delegating the things I dislike or the very best work and opportunities?
- How do I speak of others in their absence?
- How important are the people who are not yet here when I'm making this decision?
- What is the true intent of our environmental, social and governance activities?
- When my feelings rise, do I talk to everyone about how I'm experiencing the issue, or do I think first about how they might be feeling?

Strengthening Our Convictions

It's the quality of our decisions that matters the most, not necessarily the speed. Quality requires some level of courage — doing the right thing when there's a potential personal consequence. To strengthen our convictions, we can choose to invest proper time and effort in clarifying our vision for the future and the purpose of our companies. We can — and must — continually hone our character, being sure of our values and practicing them every day. We can't excuse ourselves from living our values, even for a moment. Accidents might happen, but excuses are deliberate choices.

Practically, we can use our values as a filter through which we pass all our demanding decisions, literally writing our values down and using them to test our options and choices. It's essential that we draw other people's perspectives into our thinking. We can literally place ourselves in their environment, walk the floor, meet in person and invite their perspectives. We can choose to place self-serving motives in submission to the needs and desires of others.

The beginning of moral courage is making choices with deep conviction, but the second vital element is to implement this with compassion.

THE LEADERS BOOK

Compassion — action-propelled by empathy in the service of others — overcomes the potential limitations of empathy alone.

Chapter 2
Morally Courageous Leaders
Implement with Compassion

Dave, the owner and CEO of a design business had reached maximum frustration with one of his designers, Richard. Dave felt he'd tolerated poor timeliness, low grade technical work and sulkiness for long enough and was poised to fire Richard. "I want him out and out by Monday" he told me one Wednesday at lunch. "Does Richard have any idea that this is coming?" I asked. "No," Dave admitted. "But anyone with an ounce of common sense should know!"

What had, in fact, happened over the prior two years was this: Dave had been very accommodating, empathetic to Richard's struggles both at work and at home. He had helped Richard practically many times over, never explaining the impact on him or the business nor setting expectations for improvement. Now, Dave's patience had ended abruptly. It was clear that he was resolute in his decision to remove Richard from his business. "How can you do that with compassion?" was my challenge to Dave. The tone of our conversation relaxed, Dave subsequently met with Richard and over a gentle conversation agreed a supportive exit, including financial support and connections with employers that would be potentially better for Richard. After an initial day of upset, Richard returned after the weekend visibly relieved and expressed genuine gratitude to Dave for the decision and how he had implemented it.

Without compassion, a courageous, high conviction decision can be destructive. All empathy and no action can also be destructive. Dave nearly exhibited both in his relationship with Richard. Having spent two years over-helping Richard, Dave narrowly avoided creating a bad ending to their work together, which had the potential for an unfair dismissal case and unsettling the remaining team members ("If he can do that to Richard, will he do that to me?").

Compassion is the quality that transforms a firm, hard decision into an organic one; one that leads to growth, vitality, respect and trust. Without compassion, our strong convictions and tough choices can make us hard-hearted. With compassion, our robust beliefs create opportunities for growth.

Sympathy, Empathy, Compassion

Much has been written on the need for leaders to be empathetic. We agree, mostly. We take this idea one step further and propose that leaders need to be not only empathetic but compassionate.

We can consider it like this: Sympathy is the emotion that feels for others. I have sympathy for the suffering experienced by some of my friends as well as for communities in the world that I'll never meet. Neither may be aware of my sympathetic feelings. Sympathy requires little or no action. It may be argued that feelings of sympathy can be self-orientated; *my* feelings about *your* situation become the focus of attention.

Empathy places us in the other person's shoes. We can choose to understand the emotions associated with the situation from their perspective. We feel *with* them, not just for them. Whilst empathy might be informed to an extent by our own experiences, the empathetic leader senses what the other person or parties are experiencing and feeling. In the context of leadership, empathy is most usually understood as a good, heartfelt quality and presumes that the empathic leader will make choices that benefit others. That's a very good style of leadership: we like it.

However, there are risks to being empathetic.

We find it easier to be empathetic with people who are like us. Perhaps because of our evolutionary development, our instinct to be a valued part of our tribe makes our feelings of affiliation, warmth and altruism instinctively easier with people like us. Of itself, that's not necessarily a bad thing — empathising with our family, friends and close colleagues can foster valuable, lasting bonds. The problem arises when we begin to exclude other people from our empathetic feelings, i.e. those who are less like us. They may need and value our support. They may possess perspectives that could inject valuable insight into our choices: especially regarding potentially negative consequences from our decisions. However, we may be less alert to them. The quality of our decisions are lessened by our lack of attention.

Empathy can also cause us to overvalue one person or a small group over the larger, greater good. The person or small group of people that evoke the strongest feelings, those we know and understand the most, get our attention over and above those with whom we're less empathetic.

Empathy with other people's pain can become a source of burnout. Sitting alongside and feeling with people might provide some comfort to them, but it won't necessarily solve their problems. We can then become a sponge for a lot of people's suffering, feeling the weight of it but not moving on from it.

It's also possible to be empathetic and act in self-interest. The manipulator does this very well. They understand others, experience other's feelings and then use that knowledge in the pursuit of self-interest. They keep their friends close and their enemies even closer. Con artists — experts in deceit — may be some of the most empathetic people we encounter.

Empathy on its own is therefore not quite enough.

Compassion is the desire to *act* on empathetic feelings in a way that genuinely helps the other person or people. It's a tangible expression of goodwill, of love, towards people who are suffering. Compassion propels action that is others-centric. It's more than a feeling of sympathy. It's more than an understanding of others' experiences. It's the motivation to act selflessly to help; to make a positive difference that will go some way towards resolving their pain and struggle. It's helping in their way (not necessarily our way) and doing something that actually helps *them*. Empathy is a good start, but it takes compassion to make a real and lasting positive difference in the lives of other people.

Compassion — action-propelled by empathy in the service of others — overcomes the potential limitations of empathy alone. Compassion will:

- compel us to consider the broad and wide impact of our decisions; not just the interests of our closest allies,
- cause us to seek to bring our people together and welcome diverse perspectives,
- foster creativity and recognise the multitude of needs in our teams, customers and communities and seeking to solve each of them; rather than applying monotone, uniform policies and products,
- release us from the burden of carrying too much of other people's pain. Action is integral to compassion,
- prevent us from becoming hard-hearted, manipulative leaders.

Just because we can doesn't mean that we should.

It's impossible to act in a way that is both ruthless and compassionate at the same time. We fundamentally challenge the ruthless businessperson/leader stereotype. For much of the 1980s and 1990s, received management wisdom elevated the domineering approach; the boss asserts, tells, imposes his will over everyone else in the pursuit of efficiency, shareholder returns and winning. An approach to management that is wholly objective, devoid of the human impact and interested solely in the utilitarian factors (numbers, efficiencies, technical data, algorithms, chemical compositions etc.) is indicative of brutal, domineering and hasty leadership. Money might be made, the opposition may be eliminated and efficiency extracted but very possibly at the expense of honour, justice, truth, integrity and defending the helpless (the very things that make any person *good*). A good leader is first a good person. All else flows from there.

Compassion injects the human element with a desire to act in a way that alleviates suffering. By all means we should control our tasks, but our people are there to be led, not controlled. A compassionate stance transforms a controlling attitude to one that enables people to flourish; the essence of excellent leadership.

To consider an extreme illustration: Terrorists arguably possess high conviction. They're (presumably) very clear and determined about the choices that they're making. It is, however, difficult to argue that they possess compassion. Closer to more normal scenarios, when we need to restructure our organisations, the attitude that underpins *how* we act is a strong indicator of our compassion or lack of it.

The Leadership Challenge

This leads us to one of the most significant challenges for leaders: Our decisions are often the source of some people's pain and yet our compassion can be the source of easing their distress (even if they don't recognise the latter). Tough decisions are tough precisely because of this conundrum. A decision with no meaningful negative impact is an easy one. Leaders don't become leaders on the strength of easy choices! Most are faced with decisions that feel more like choosing between bad and worse or a rock and a hard place. It takes strength to lead with compassion. It's not the soft option — far from it! Caring about the impact of tough choices on a wide range of people and acting to lessen their struggles takes keen intelligence and determined effort.

Industry leaders know this to be true. It's easier to dump waste than to treat it properly, to cut employee numbers quickly than ride out a soft market and to squeeze suppliers rather than support them. Third sector leaders know this to be true. The CEO of a homeless charity described to us the complexities of being compassionate when evicting someone from one of their shelters: "It's easy to just kick them out, but removing them compassionately takes more thought."

Excellent leaders work hard to hold these tensions together and the indicators that we look for when assessing for compassion could be as follows:

- Referring to people as "people," not as headcount (which sounds more like cattle to us) or even as resources. Compassionate leaders allow themselves to consider the real people they're involved with, embrace the emotions that might arise from hard choices and refuse to disguise the pain inflicted with euphemisms.

    - Leaders "walk the floor." They go where their people are, experience what their people experience; they're not ensconced in a C-suite.

    - A variety of people contribute to structured leadership discussions. The team is itself diverse.

Representatives from across the business contribute. Leaders listen to learn.

- The communities that the organisation operates in are considered in leadership team meetings. We observe "community impact" or similar on the agenda. This isn't about salving conscience through charity or promotional photo opportunities. It's a genuine desire to alleviate suffering in their communities.

- Reports that indicate weaker morale, complaints, health and safety failings and negative environmental impact are considered and valued, not dismissed.

- Doing the right thing is discussed in priority to avoiding lawsuits.

It's often easier to not exercise compassion. Compassion takes strength and skill, learned through choice and practice. That's why it's so valuable.

The Case for Compassion

Just in case we haven't made the case for compassionate leadership clearly enough, hopefully the findings from research by Potential Project (referenced by Founder Rasmus Hougaard and Senior Partner Jacqueline Carter in their book, Compassionate Leadership), will do the trick. Leaders high in compassion reported sixty-three percent lower burnout, sixty-six percent lower stress and are two times less likely to want to quit their organisations than leaders low in compassion. Whilst compassion isn't self-directed in its intention, leaders clearly benefit from being compassionate people.

Compassionate leaders achieve greater career success than those who are actively self-centred. There are a number of studies that show that authentically pro-social, agreeable, generous, kind people are more likely to be promoted and have higher average earnings than their less agreeable colleagues. The research is interesting, but you might not need it; you probably know which type of character you'd prefer to promote to your team.

Moral courage — making decisions with deep conviction and implementing those decisions with compassion — is the defining hallmark of excellent leaders.

The adrenaline-addicted leader will set aside risk considerations and make reckless choices.

Chapter 3
Morally Courageous Leaders
Resist Immediate Gratification

If we're to lead others, then we first need to lead ourselves well. The quality of our lives and leadership is significantly influenced by our ability to resist temptation and immediate gratification. Our "fast thinking" instinct for self-preservation can skew our responses in our favour and create the conditions for an unhealthy (potentially immoral) action. If we want to inspire other people to live purposeful lives, to harness their unique brilliance, to be excellent, creative people who themselves inspire others, then we need to resist self-serving seductions. These distractions nearly always make intuitive sense in the immediate moment and yet with even a few seconds of reflection, we know we are poised for error: a choice that will set us up to disappoint the people we care about and potentially for disaster.

The slippery path to immediate gratification can creep up on us unnoticed, like the proverbial frog not realising that he's slowly boiling to death in a pot on the stove as the temperature gradually increases. There are four observable temptations that give us clues as to whether we're in the pot and need to jump out — fast!

The Temptation to Quit

Leadership is for the long haul. It's more like an endurance race than a sprint. In any endurance event, the temptation to give up is real. If you've attempted to run a marathon, you may have encountered "the wall." This occurs around the twenty mile mark (for me it was 18) when stored glycogen is depleted and muscle performance deteriorates rapidly. Your mind screams "sit down" as your body gives alarming signal — perhaps reasonably! Runners, especially those of us who are amateurs, need to push through this moment if we're to finish the race.

Morally courageous leaders don't quit on their people. Have you known someone who's always got your back, who encourages you constantly and who cheers you on? Chances are that they've made a strong, positive impact on you. That's the power of moral courage.

There's a caveat to come (temptation four), but faithfully supporting other people is a hallmark of an excellent leader. They push through the temptation to give up on their people and instead press on together towards their objectives.

What can cause us to want to give up on people?

- They're not fast enough. Using our marathon analogy, the morally courageous leader wants everyone to cross the finish line, not just themselves. It's "our" race, not "my" race. It's a human race not a solo expedition. One of the most common reasons that people fail to complete a marathon is that they've started out too fast.

Leaders who expect excessive speed from their people will burn them out and leave them at the side of the road. There's a race to be run, but unless you're a professional athlete, it shouldn't be at Olympic medal speed.

- They're not good enough. That might be true; others in the team might not yet be as competent as the leader would like. The short-term leader will quickly change their team and forget about those they've moved out. The courageous leader will encourage and stretch their people to learn and grow. It will take time, but that's OK because this is a long race, not a sprint.

- The conditions aren't perfect. The ideal conditions for running a marathon in my amateur view include a flat course, light rain and no wind. If I wait for such conditions, chances are I'll never run a mile — let alone a marathon! Not-ideal conditions will provoke "short-termist" leaders to give up on their objectives and their people rather than persist and adapt.

The Temptation to be Careless

Have you ever found yourself poised to break healthy habits in order to cross a boundary? "I know I should do/say this but right now I just can't be bothered." Or perhaps you find yourself tempted to let someone down: "I need to get this done so I'll skip that meeting I'm supposed to be at." Or for some, it's the impulse to jump in and argue in every conversation: "I'm only being honest, so I'll give them a piece of my mind."

These are examples of self-sabotaging behaviour. It's careless, undermines relationships and compromises quality. It's a habit that will fracture the strength of your leadership and inject compromise to your role modelling.

There are many ways that impulsive behaviour plays out to the point of carelessness. In our experience these are the most frequent. Do any resonate with you?

"I have too much to do."

Being active is a good thing. Being excessively busy isn't. There's a seduction to busyness. The need to be needed, to be seen as important, can be associated with excessive activity. The foundation for carelessness is laid when work becomes too much of a source of self-identity. We skip healthy habits — including eating at lunchtime. We stop taking even short breaks during the day. Someone once told me they didn't have time to go to the toilet between meetings (crazy!). We drop out of commitments that don't serve our own agendas, including catch-ups with colleagues, coffee dates with people who don't have an immediate benefit to us; even family occasions will be sacrificed. All so that we can attend instead to the client email, board pack and latest problem that's arisen at work.

The excessively busy person will console themselves that it's worth it: they feel that they're a high achiever and so they jump thoughtlessly to the next task. In reality, the sacrifices in their relationships are disproportionate to the benefits and will compromise their long-term success. After all, who wants to be around someone who's too busy to pay us any proper attention?

"I'm right; they're wrong."

Some leaders are more naturally disposed towards outbursts than others. The impulsive, careless leader excuses those outbursts and believes that others should "just deal with it."

We jump in and interrupt in every conversation; asserting our views before other people have had a chance to fully express theirs. We use strong language (sometimes bad language), to underscore the importance of our perspectives. We might even actively undermine others, telling tales, using disrespectful euphemisms about them ("'Sleepy Joe' won't deliver his numbers") as a way to elevate ourselves. We might send messages riddled with typos as frustration and haste overtake us.

The excuse is that we're being honest, but in fact we're being arrogant. We're choosing not to listen nor to learn and instead we impulsively respond and assert our opinions and choices.

The curious observation is that we might be right in our opinion, but it won't matter because we've expressed ourselves so carelessly that others won't want to follow.

"I'm achieving great results, so I deserve a break."

We're all for breaks. It's important to take care of ourselves; to rest, recover and recharge. However, when a sense of entitlement creeps in, "breaks" become an excuse for making poor and damaging choices.

We can believe that we're doing so well that we deserve something special — something more than the average person would receive, because without us, this place would be in trouble. The tempting impulse is to flex — perhaps even break — procedures, policies and common-sense boundaries.

For example, we might excuse a few extra drinks on the company credit card or bump ourselves up to business class even though policy is for premium economy. Or we'd take the morning off without telling anyone ("After all, I won a massive new account last week!"). These are decisions that are made in seconds but that will impact on our reputation for years.

To repeat, it's not taking a break that's the problem. It's the self-centred sense of entitlement. It's an attitude that conveys to others that they're somehow lesser, not important, that they don't really matter. That the person who truly matters is me.

Resisting this temptation requires actively engaging with your team rather than becoming isolated. Ask for permission or tell them what you intend to do. You can also flip the situation. If someone else in your team took the action that you're poised to take, how would you feel? That pause might be just enough to prevent a dishonourable choice.

"I need to take this on to get ahead in my career."

Some of us are masters at curating our reputation (or at least, we think we are). Early in our careers taking on responsibility after responsibility can help propel us forward.

When we take on responsibilities that we can't actually handle — whether because we have too much on already or we're not yet competent — we can achieve the very opposite and undermine our reputation. We've taken on responsibility, but we're not actually responsible — we're careless.

Committing to something feels great in that moment; others are grateful and hopeful. That gives us a sense of immediate pleasure. However, we're judged by our actions and not by our intentions. If we don't deliver and fail to follow through, we'll damage our good standing. In more acute cases, we might even develop a reputation for letting people down.

If you're one of life's impulsive volunteers, here's a phrase that'll help you: "Let me think about that and I'll get back to you." Give yourself a chance to pause — even if only for a few moments so that you can consider your resources. If, with proper consideration, you're able to reallocate and make some time, then great — go for it!

The Temptation to be a Hero

More accurately, this is the temptation to start a fire and then heroically put it out. Arson is both destructive and illegal. Yet many leaders commit the equivalent of arson in their companies and burn themselves and others in the process.

The adrenaline-addicted leader will set aside risk considerations and make reckless choices. The problem is that they don't believe that they're being reckless. They think that they're somehow superhuman and they bask in the perceived glory of saving the day. What they fail to realise is that the day only needed to be saved because of their reckless bravado.

There's a difference between courage — doing the right thing due to having weighed the risks — and bravado. Bravado is "a show of courage, especially when unnecessary and dangerous, to make people admire you."

Why might we be tempted towards such unnecessary danger? Consider the following faulty beliefs:

"No pain; no gain."

Whilst it's sometimes true that achieving outstanding results often takes discipline and some sacrifices, it's not always true. We can achieve some great wins sometimes without putting ourselves through pain and stress. The high-bravado leader doesn't believe this and under-appreciates the simpler successes. Worse, they actively seek out stresses and pain as a way to validate their own sense of importance.

We observe this in leaders who work excessive hours believing that it's the only way to get results and be admired. Some will attempt to do their most important work late at night, believing that tiredness doesn't affect them, but only others (who are weaker). They're wrong, of course, but they don't see the problem.

"I perform better when under pressure."

All fake news has a modicum of truth to it. In this case, it's true that some level of pressure can quicken our senses, strengthen our resolve and catalyse creativity. Excessive and chronic stress, however, will achieve the very opposite: dulled senses, decision dithering and a poverty of new ideas.

Associating high levels of pressure with high levels of performance will result in decisions that create high-pressure conditions; often pointlessly. Our frequently-encountered example is the way that some leaders leave it until the very last moment to prepare for something important — a shareholder presentation, major client pitch, tough negotiation or a critical meeting with a colleague. They could choose to prepare way in advance, but that would feel less pressurised than leaving it late and the leader therefore (wrongly) believes that the result will be inferior. Rather than prepare, review, involve others and improve the report, the leader rushes (often frustrated and frustrating others) at the last moment. The idea that the event will be better because of the stress associated with leaving it to the last moment is simply not true. In fact, quite the opposite.

"I could do this blindfolded."

Over-confidence will lead to self-inflicted blindness. Rather than inviting challenge, seeking out answers and looking for evidence, the over-confident leader asserts their decisions with little or no data. They take pride in their belief that they can do practically anything because they're simply better than most (or all) other people. It's like driving with our eyes closed: sooner or later, there will be a crash.

The Temptation to Blame-Shift

Unless you're exceptionally lucky, you'll have experienced some problems in your life. You might even have made a mistake or two along the way. For most of us, when things are going wrong, we're tempted to shift the blame away from ourselves: "It's not my fault; they made me do it."

Weak leaders get stuck and blame other people or circumstances for their troubles. They're immersed with problems and are unwilling to solve them. This leader believes that others are either not capable or not interested in playing their part and so they assume a quiet woe: "I'll just have to take another hit for the team." This quickly builds into resentment — a desperately unhealthy attitude both for them and those they interact with. They're terrible delegators, perhaps allocating responsibility once but then taking it back the instant that someone is perceived to have let them down. They don't hold others to account: suffering quietly in silence whilst the resentment grows and grows.

In other words, they shift the blame for their problems onto others rather than take responsibility and make changes.

Someone who shifts the blame will:

- Rarely ask for help or asks at the very last moment, making it difficult for others to support them,
- Stay quiet in the meeting and get vocal after the meeting,
- Hint and assume that others know what the issues are rather than raise the problem clearly and directly,
- Hoard the important work. The team aren't trusted with important priorities,

- Email badly: late at night, they might copy in bosses when making a point and write without empathy,
- Say "I'm fine" when they're frustrated,
- Let other people off the hook and become quietly annoyed that they have to take on that person's responsibilities,
- Be quietly angry at having to sacrifice personal or family occasions because an issue has been "dumped" on them,
- Erupt in anger at something minor because of having simmered for weeks over a difficult conversation or issue.

The resentment associated with a blame-shift mentality eventually leaves a deeply negative impression on others. It's a form of pride.

Resist Temptation

When we're tired and stressed (i.e. beyond stretched), we're more susceptible to succumb to any of these temptations. What will help us to resist?

- Refuel. It's essential to drink water when running a marathon. It's extremely helpful to take on fuel, glucose and sugars too. Actively seek encouragement and support, ask for it rather than expect it to arrive unsolicited. Spend more time with people who energise you and less (much less) with mood-hoovers — those who suck the life out of you.

Make time for fun: schedule in the people and activity that you enjoy.

- Recover. In athletics, recovery is essential to achieving muscle growth. In the same way, recovery is essential to our personal and leadership growth. Make time to recover. Take a break every day. Take your holidays (properly). Set aside time every month away from work to think.

- Reinvigorate your relationships. When tempted to quit on your people, it's time to reinvigorate those relationships. Invest time (quality time) with them. Revisit the purpose of your work with colleagues. Pay proper attention. Put your phone away. Linger with people rather than rush. Eat together.

Moral courage demands that we resist the seduction of immediate gratification. What can you do to resist temptation, starting from today?

THE LEADERS BOOK

Moral integrity ensures that we do the right thing even when it's not the easiest thing.

Chapter 4
Morally Courageous Leaders
Do the Right Thing

When seven lives were taken in 1982, after the consumption of the Extra-Strength Tylenol painkiller capsules that had been laced with cyanide, drugmakers Johnson & Johnson were faced with the most tragic of circumstances. It's been one of the most talked about and written about case studies — not just because of the tragedy itself, but the way in which Johnson & Johnson handled it. What could've led to the utter ruin of the company, in fact lead to the enhancement of a strong and robust reputation. Johnson & Johnson emerged as a company of integrity. But why?

When people were predicting that this sabotage would ultimately end Tylenol, a brand that accounted for a sizeable percentage of Johnson & Johnson's net income, what was it that Johnson & Johnson did to turn things around and gain a reputation of integrity?

They put the customer first: they were honest with the general public and they took responsibility though it wasn't their fault. They recalled all the Tylenol painkillers and gave free replacement products to people. They took immediate action. They did the right thing.

If we're going to be morally courageous then we're going to have to have integrity. We are going to have to do the right thing. We have to do the right thing just because it's exactly that: the right thing. We don't do it, because it's going to make us look good or it's going to benefit us in some way.

Integrity by its very definition encompasses having strong moral principles. But possessing strong moral principles is one thing; sticking by them is another. And it's in the uncompromising adherence to those principles that integrity is demonstrated. To be a person of integrity, we must be honest and live honestly.

Integrity is the state or quality of being undivided or complete. It ensures that there's no divide between the person you're in public and the person you're in private. There should be a continuation and a completion of character throughout all aspects of our lives.

Moral courage and integrity go hand in hand. Neither one solely drives the other. It takes moral courage to choose to do the right thing even when it costs dearly, and it takes integrity to choose to be morally courageous. Together they form the very foundation of great leadership. Integrity matters!

Your Authentic Self - Personal Integrity

When it comes to our personal integrity, it really is all about being yourself and being comfortable with who you are. It's about being authentic. To be secure in one's own skin for some of us can be difficult as self-confidence doesn't come naturally and sometimes we're tempted to be someone we're not in order to fit in. Whilst we should never feel the need to do this, there's a vast difference between this type of feeling and the chameleon style character that just changes with every setting. Personal integrity requires that there's no pretence. We're not trying to be anyone or anything other than who or what we are and at times that may mean that we stand out and that we're radically different from everyone else, because we're being true to ourselves and being led by our principles and values; not led by the crowd.

Personal integrity asks that we be honest with ourselves. The self-aware leader also recognises that the average human being is very good at lying to themselves at times. We tend to do this not out of some desire to be dishonest but because we quite reasonably want to avoid negative emotions and feelings of pain. We lie to ourselves about ourselves, because we don't really want to deal with characteristics or traits we wish we didn't have. We also often tell lies to ourselves about our situations, work and relationships because if we're really honest, we'd need to do something to change those things. We do it in a sense to protect ourselves for self-preservation.

This lying to ourselves comes out in different ways. We find ourselves being defensive because we actually know that there's truth in what is being told to us. We can often be overly critical or judgemental of behaviours because we see this in ourselves. We get caught up in things that will distract us from reality, we get irrationally angry with the things that really don't matter because the things that really do matter are too overwhelming to deal with.

How easy it is to say something arrogant when we feel intimidated; to say something hurtful when we're feeling deep hurt! Or we can often make an insensitive comment or inappropriate joke because we feel awkward in the present situation.

Of course, all these things will create barriers between others and ourselves, and threatens to damage our integrity with our people. Being honest with ourselves about why we act and react in the way we do is a great starting point to enabling our integrity to blossom. Moral courage is about looking at ourselves and seeing ourselves for who we really are. Personal integrity helps us to look beyond the immediate and go deeper; to engage in honest reflection.

Principled - Ethical Integrity

The difference between ethical and moral integrity is that where ethical integrity is abiding by the rules and regulations and upholding the law, moral integrity is holding fast to your values that are at the core of your being. Great leaders and great organisations are law-abiding and adhere to societal rules. In doing so, respect for the dignity of others is then given. If we're to be governed by ethical principles, then we'll have to care about justice and a sense of fairness throughout all of our policies and procedures. This also includes not being content with living in the fog of ignorance. Too many companies are found wanting when it comes to ethical practices.

However, moral courage will demand at times that we go far beyond ethical integrity in order to do the right thing. There's a requirement to act with ethical *and* moral integrity. After all, the famous Titanic passenger ship set sail abiding by the Board of Trade laws. But twenty lifeboats for two thousand two hundred passengers — by anyone's standard — is not sufficient. With only space for half of the passengers, one thousand five hundred people tragically lost their lives. The law was outdated; but is this an adequate justification? Of course not. Our actions may be legal, but do they promote good, strong moral values? When our people can see that we've the moral courage to act with complete integrity, they'll afford us the dedication and trust we desire and we in turn demonstrate our commitment to them.

Values Led - Moral Integrity

Moral integrity ensures that we do the right thing even when it's not the easiest thing. Integrity has no regard for how hard or painful a choice is. This is why moral courage is needed, because popularity, promotion and profit can all threaten to trump integrity at times; moral courage screams integrity.

A key component of integrity is to be led and guided by our values. Our values should influence all that we do and are and the decisions we make. This incorporates both our personal lives, professional lives and the life of the organisation. There should be no chasm between intentions and actions. All that we do should be aligned with our company's purpose and values. Integrity must be one of the most widespread values that organisations have in their mission statements and fixed on their walls, but integrity can only be a core value if we really are living out the aim, purpose and values our business adheres to.

Integrity isn't just introspective. Rather, it requires us to understand how we fit into the team and organisation.

Integrity means that we think of others and consider how we interact with others. Integrity involves staying true to our word, being honest and truthful and being consistent in our actions and behaviours whoever we are with and wherever we are.

Open Your Mind - Intellectual Integrity

Our shining example with regards to intellectual integrity is of course the father of philosophy: Socrates. He was passionate and driven in the pursuit of truth, even under attack and adversity and right up until his tragic end. Intellectual integrity will spur us on to discover the truth, learn the facts, know all of the situation and try to reach the best decision we can. It means that we won't ignore evidence, but rather that we'll actively and courageously seek it out.

Leaders who have high integrity are in constant learning mode. They recognise that they've never arrived and there's always more to know and more to discover. They're honest with themselves and they seek out guidance and help to improve on their areas of stretch. They're open to change and willing to make mistakes and admit to them. They've understood that mistakes can be a springboard for success.

Intellectual integrity is found within honest feedback: both in the giving of it to others and in the openness to receive it (integrity is truthful and is a pursuit of truth). As we've read, the transparent leader doesn't shy away from giving honest feedback, even if it might be hard for a person to receive. Why? Because in fact, integrity doesn't say one thing when it means another.

Integrity Spreads

We must always lead in the way we wish to be led and the way we wish our people to live. If integrity matters to us in others, then it must matter to the standards we place on our own lives and companies. Integrity should permeate our organisations, but that starts with the leader.

Are we living a complete and undivided existence? Can we be trusted in all things at all times, even when the eyes of the world aren't upon us? Like the Buddhist monk who wanted to teach his students a moral lesson by asking them to steal from the wealthy when no-one was looking, we should be like the student who's recognised that there's nowhere we can ever go where we won't be seen — we will always see ourselves.

*Don't talk about it;
do something about it.*

Chapter 5
Morally Courageous Leaders
Embrace the Defining Moments

A defining moment. When there's a before and an after. Change occurs, sometimes quickly and sometimes over a longer period. But there's change; you change. This takes moral courage.

Sometimes the change is a shift in direction or in purpose. Sometimes it's a moment of revelation, a truth realised that can't be unknown; sometimes it comes to refine what's already in us.

Joseph Badaracco, Professor of Business Ethics at Harvard Business School, says that defining moments have three characteristics: they reveal, they test and they shape.

So, a defining moment could seem small but have a significant impact. Think of something that someone said to you that resonated so deeply, you had to act on it (for example, the young student being told by their French teacher that they'd never get a good grade in their A-level). Perhaps there's some evidence for the teacher saying this, maybe the student wasn't great at French or maybe they didn't enjoy it and struggled in the lessons. Yet their dream was to go to university and therefore to do well in their studies — even if they weren't enjoying them all. And so that student took those words and used them to focus their efforts — to remind themselves what the bigger goal was. And, true story, as a result, they ultimately achieved a B grade in French — far from the fail that had been predicted. Whilst we don't recommend this approach to teaching, it did reveal the potential reality of the situation and it did test the student's resolve. Let's face it, they could've given up having received the teacher's criticism, but instead it shaped their determination and action.

This also reminds us that as leaders we need to be mindful of our words. Whether you are a parent, teacher, CEO, religious leader; what you say, even if not significant to you, may be more significant than you realise to those around you. Perhaps you've had someone recount a time when you said something to them that particularly encouraged, helped or challenged them in a positive way. Perhaps you have little or no recollection of the conversation, because to you it was an ordinary conversation. Our words matter: let's use them wisely.

A defining moment could also be a dramatic one. In 1992, Kees van der Graaf's life changed forever when his young son was diagnosed with a type of muscular dystrophy for which there was no cure. Kees went on to dedicate his life to finding a cure for this particular disease, eventually retiring early from a senior executive role in Unilever, in order to fully focus on his life's purpose. A personal, family crisis led to a complete shift in direction for Kees, a discovery of new purpose and a determination to go after the goal.

For Such a Time as This

Some defining moments come and they're exactly what we've been training or working our whole life for. One well-known example of this was in 2009 when pilot Chesley Burnett "Sully" Sullenberger III (a retired American fighter pilot and then airline pilot), successfully landed US Airways Flight 1549 in the Hudson River after both engines were disabled by a bird strike shortly after take-off. All one hundred and fifty-five people aboard survived and newspaper headlines heralded the event "Miracle on the Hudson." Moral courage at its finest.

Sullenberger had to be quick to assess that he would be unable to reach any nearby airports and that the emergency landing on water was the best option. He didn't make this decision in a "gung-ho" manner — he describes how he felt as they were about to land as "the worst sickening, pit-of-your-stomach, falling-through-the-floor feeling" that he had ever experienced. Sullenberger was last off the plane, leaving only after making certain that all passengers had made it off.

On reflection, Sullenberger also said: "One way of looking at this might be that for forty-two years, I've been making small, regular deposits in this bank of experience, education and training. And on 15 January, the balance was sufficient so that I could make a very large withdrawal." Sullenberger didn't invite the moment or have it as a life goal, but all those daily decisions, daily practices, knowledge and experience led up to him being able to save the lives of one hundred and fifty-five people.

The recent Covid pandemic is another defining moment for Dr Nicola Brink, Director of Public Health, Guernsey, Channel Islands. Dr Brink quickly became a household name for anyone living in the Bailiwick of Guernsey during the pandemic. We had the privilege of being in conversation with Dr Brink as we were curious about the leadership qualities and skills that she cultivated before the pandemic.

Dr Brink shared with us a moment that changed the course of her career. Whilst she was living in South Africa, training to be a haematologist, she noticed that many patients were experiencing complications following bone marrow transplantation and dying of viral infections. Dr Brink remembers going to see the Professor of Virology at the University of Cape Town and saying that she really thought there should be more done to diagnose viral infections, especially as there were effective antiviral therapies being developed at the time. Dr Brink remembers he turned to her and said "Don't talk about it; do something about it. Become a virologist." This resonated so much with Dr Brink and has transformed how she's approached almost every problem since. She felt compelled to not just identify the problem, but contribute to the solution. People generally can be very good at identifying problems when things aren't working, but that isn't the time to sit back and wait for someone else to resolve or fix it. That professor's words changed Dr Brink's focus and is the reason she became a virologist. Shortly afterwards, the HIV epidemic broke out and she became involved in HIV care in South Africa.

Fast forward a number of years to 2003, when Dr Brink arrived in Guernsey with her family. She started life in

Guernsey by taking a career break to spend time with her children. But by the time Covid19 arrived, Dr Brink was Director of Public Health in the Bailiwick. In November 2019 Dr Brink led a tabletop exercise to simulate Guernsey's response in the event of a pandemic. At the time there was pressure to cancel the exercise as some parties felt there were other priorities and other more pressing risks to the island community. But Dr Brink had done the research, she knew her subject matter and she had the courage of her convictions to stand firm. She remembers saying to other decision makers, "It's not a case of if it happens; it's when it happens and we are overdue a pandemic." That courage to stand by her decision, in the face of challenge and scepticism, was undoubtedly a defining moment for the Bailiwick community. Just weeks later, Covid19 was identified in Wuhan, China. By the end of January 2020, the World Health Organisation (WHO) declared it a Public Health Emergency of International Concern and on 11 March 2020, they further declared the outbreak as a pandemic.

One of the key findings as a result of the planning exercise was the need to communicate clearly. This might sound obvious to many, but we know in leadership there can be a strong temptation to heavily filter information, control the narrative and at times "spin" the facts and their implications or minimise them — often with good intentions but almost always driven by our own fear and insecurity. However, Dr Brink and her team made the conscious and courageous decision right at the start of the pandemic that there would be no public health spokesperson. They recognised that due to the severity of the situation, the community needed to see the face of public health, and as Dr Brink says "we had to be accountable for our decision making. We couldn't hide behind anonymity." Dr Brink may not express it in this way, but in all her training and experience, she had built on a core value of truth and honesty and was driven by the need to help to solve the problem. It wasn't just about identifying it or simply to tell others about it, but to actually do something about it. Dr Brink lived her values and her values informed all her decision making.

It's the Preparation that Counts

In all these stories: from the student facing exam failure, Sullenberger landing a passenger plane in the river and Dr Brink guiding a community through the pandemic, there are some common threads in each one.

Firstly, there is clear vision and goals. We have to get the grades to go to university, land the plane, save lives and work together to protect an island community from a pandemic.

Secondly, these stories demonstrate how these individuals drew on their internal resources to achieve their goals. The student focussed their thinking and put in extra effort even though they didn't enjoy the subject. The pilot's focus intensified: he was able to assess the situation, activate all his training and experience and take appropriate and timely action. The virologist, already aware of the risks, prioritised preparation and training of key teams, lived her values and remained firm and focused under challenge and scrutiny while empowering and equipping others.

And lastly, these stories show how each person responded to pressure. This is when the first two themes above are tested. We all have a choice about how we respond to being under pressure: whether it's exam pressure, personal tragedy, unexpected workplace or community crisis. How do we show up? Do we show up?

We can't help but think about the formation of diamonds at this point — no doubt familiar to us all. We know that diamonds were formed billions of years ago, about one hundred miles below the surface of the Earth from carbon atoms and that the conditions in which they formed required intense heat and pressure. Diamonds took varying time frames to form: it could've been days, weeks, months or even millions of years. What is fascinating is that the process of growing diamonds wasn't necessarily continuous. It could be interrupted, for example, if there was a change in conditions (like pressure or temperature) and then when conditions were right, the diamonds would begin to grow again.

As leaders we need to recognise our defining moments. Remember, Joseph Badaracco, says that defining moments have three characteristics: they reveal, they test, and they shape. We use the imagery that goes with the formation of diamonds to give us a healthy perspective. If we allow them to, our defining moments (times when we face pressure and heat) can cultivate something incredibly precious, valuable and rare. As leaders we must continually be on the lookout for our defining moments and what we can learn from them; how we can grow.

So, what will you do with your defining moments? How are you preparing yourself for them? Dr Brink is an ordinary person who helped to guide a community safely and skilfully through a pandemic, making tough decisions that weren't always popular. However, she was able to do that as a result of developing her character and her skills over the course of her life; moment by moment. Similarly, with Sullenberger, he recognised his skills and his character and both were shaped over decades. When the ultimate defining moment came, he was able to draw on them under the most intense pressure and with the most incredible outcome.

Defining moments may not be moments that we would choose — by nature they're a test (uncomfortable and even painful), but great leaders meet them head on. Great leaders don't shrink back. They're morally courageous in the face of great challenge. What do you need to face head on today?

THE LEADERS BOOK

ns book

Authentic Trust

THE LEADERS BOOK

Foreword
Trustworthy Leaders
Matt Bird, Business and Social Entrepreneur

Trust and authenticity is a hallmark of any truly good person, regardless of their rank and role in an organisation. Trust is an essential foundation of any team or company that's worthy of our time, attention and money.

Trust is built through consistent performance. A leader who consistently delivers results gains trust. A team who consistently does what they say they're going to do, grows trust. A business that consistently provides amazing products or services, builds trust.

The other powerful way to build trust is through the non-transactional dimensions of a relationship. Most of our human interactions in the average working day are transactional: we're communicating with people because they're doing something for us or we're doing something for them or we're doing something together. There's nothing wrong with transactional relationships, however the non-transactional dimensions in a relationship build incredible trust. Showing we care about people and not only what they can do for us, builds a whole different level of authentic trust.

How great do you feel when someone you know takes the trouble to reach out simply to see how you're doing? As it was once said, being heard and being loved are so close that most people can't tell the difference. Genuinely caring about people and not just what they can do for you, builds untold levels of authentic trust.

One of my life mantras is "stop networking and start relationships." I find networking contrived, manipulative and disingenuous because it's all about what you can "get" from people. Contrastingly, relationships are about building trust through which both parties grow. This is what I call Relationology — the art and science of authentic, high-trust and long-term relationships.

PublishU — my most recent business venture — coaches people to write a book in 100-days and then publish it globally. At the beginning of the course, I explain that eight out of ten students complete the course with a manuscript for their book and the key to being one of the eight is trust!

To achieve their goal, my students need to trust themselves: this won't be the first time they've trusted themselves to achieve something new. Secondly, I invite students to trust me as their coach: I've written twenty books and coached hundreds of people every year; so, I have powerful insights to share. Finally, to trust the "Writing My Book"process: it's a tried-and-tested course that enables hundreds of people a year to become published authors. The whole business is built on trust. I'd claim that the success of any business is built on trust.

LEADERS are passionate about helping leaders build authentic trust that drives performance and success. In the chapters that follow they provide insights into how we can all build authentic trust in our leadership, teams and organisations.

THE LEADERS BOOK

Transparency is key because it helps people to trust what we say.

Chapter 6
Trustworthy Leaders
Don't Hide

Great leaders don't hide. Instead, they demonstrate transparency.

We know that trust is hard-won and easily lost.

As leaders how do we know when we have the trust of our people, our stakeholders and our clients? What do we see and what do we hear? Maybe more importantly, what do they see in our behaviours as leaders? Transparency is the first of five principles that we believe are essential for leaders to build trust. What do we mean by transparency and how does that translate into action and behaviours for leaders?

We believe that transparency isn't something you do, but it's a mindset. It's a mindset that's fundamental for leaders if they're to build and maintain trust. As leaders, we need to know what to do to cultivate this mindset!

Transparency is key because it helps people to trust what we say. How do we know if a leader is demonstrating openness? What would we expect to observe and experience when we visited their organisation?

There are a number of signs and symptoms we can look out for:

- Everyone regardless of role would be clear about the organisation's vision and purpose and how they contribute to it.

- Clear context and rationale for decisions made would be shared; leaving no room for false narratives to take root.

- People would be well informed of organisational health and their future — honestly and in a straight-forward way. There'd be no exaggerating positives or minimising negatives.

- People would hear the leader telling the truth at all times and in a timely way; especially when the news is bad.

- People would know about the leader's successes and mistakes because both would be shared by the leader, not via rumour or gossip.

Whilst this is a straightforward, perhaps even obvious list, in our experience it's rarely demonstrated as well a leader intends it to be. Transparency is more challenging to deliver for some leaders compared to others, depending on their natural styles and their own personal values and beliefs.

Transparency in Action

First, let's explore one example where we've seen these aspects done well. In this case by a large, national organisation. The organisation had already identified trust in leadership as an aspect to work on and had been implementing improvements and making progress for a number of years before they were faced with a challenging organisational restructure which would result in the loss of over one hundred jobs.

The organisation's leadership team spent time not only drafting the proposed new structure but crucially planning the communications and implementation of the consultation period in great detail (significant resources were invested in this preparation phase). This meant that when the restructure was announced, it was announced to the whole organisation on the same day with messages appropriately tailored depending on the potential impact on the individual. For example, those at risk of redundancy received their own communications prior to the whole organisation communication.

The initial communications reminded people of the organisation's purpose and vision whilst clearly and concisely outlining the challenges that were being faced. Alongside this the options that had already been explored were presented and the projection was given for the situation if no changes were to be implemented.

There followed a clear timeline of organisational communications — in a variety of ways. For example, online communications, face to face meetings, regularly updated documents and emails.

During the consultation period people were encouraged to offer their own ideas and perspectives and these were responded to. Some were implemented and many were not. However, a response was given. People felt heard and therefore valued, even if their ideas were not taken forward.

In this example, you can see how senior leaders demonstrated transparency; they were clear and honest in their communication (without oversharing) and in doing so managed anxieties well. They created a space where people felt able to put forward alternative views and ideas and crucially these were responded to. People genuinely felt that the leadership were seeking the best outcome for the organisation and not just looking after those at the very top. In fact, one of the key senior individuals leading on the restructure actually removed their role from the new structure in order to better maintain frontline delivery of services. The way the process was implemented resulted in people understanding how the final decisions were arrived at and why some redundancies were necessary. Some people did have to leave the organisation, but this was done respectfully with compassion and support.

How Hard Can it Be?

If transparency is fundamental to growing trust, what do leaders need to do to cultivate it?

Being Self-Aware

Leaders need to be self-aware and comfortable in their own skin. They need to be honest with themselves before they can truly cultivate trust in their organisation. People will spot when a leader is faking it sooner or later. A leader who is self-aware, knows their own strengths, knows their areas for development, is aware of their default leadership style and how to adapt in certain situations or with different individuals. They are constantly seeking to identify their blind spots. That leader will find demonstrating transparency second nature — they won't feel like they're always performing, they can be their authentic selves in the workplace and we're living in a time when this is pivotal for people to want to follow a leader. People want to really know who they are following and be able to identify with them in some way.

Leaders need to be connected to their people. This is a common conversation in our work: if relationships are transactional, trust is limited, people become suspicious of agendas, they do not feel valued, instead they may feel used and discarded. When leaders genuinely seek to make connections with their people, genuinely seek to understand some of their life outside the workplace and how they experience life within the workplace, human connections are made, trust is built and workplaces flourish. The responsibility to grow these connections starts and ends with the leaders. Leaders set the tone and behaviours that others follow and replicate.

The Gift of Feedback

Leaders need to be honest when giving feedback. They shouldn't be brutally honest, but clear, compassionate and productive. People need truthful feedback so they can grow and develop their own skills. By not giving this kind of feedback a leader could be holding their people back, constraining them through fear of upsetting them or perhaps fear that they will flourish too quickly and overtake the knowledge or skills of that leader (this isn't something a good leader fears)! Brené Brown has explored this topic in depth, and she emphasises how "clear is kind; unclear is unkind." She goes on to describe what this can look like in the workplace:

"Feeding people half-truths or bullshit to make them feel better (which is almost always about making ourselves feel more comfortable) is unkind. Not getting clear with a colleague about your expectations because it feels too hard, yet holding them accountable or blaming them for not delivering is unkind. Talking about people rather than to them is unkind."

As leaders, it's our job to ensure this doesn't become a description of the culture in our organisation.

Leaders need to be brave — not fear-driven. Leaders need to let go of any notion that knowledge is power and therefore only for the leader: this belief has no place in healthy, transformational leadership and transparency is entirely unachievable wherever this belief is held. The best, most trustworthy leaders aren't intimidated by the prospect of sharing knowledge and power with their people. They recognise this collaborative approach is best for the organisation and for everyone involved (be that employees, clients, customers or shareholders).

Leaders need to be smart enough to know they don't need to have all the answers. The expectation that a leader has to have all the answers is at best outdated and unrealistic and at worst it's harmful and toxic. If a leader behaves like they have all the answers, they stifle the growth of the people within their organisation, motivation is depleted and innovation and creativity die. The organisation can't grow and ultimately this often leads to a loss to other competitors. The most successful leaders not only surround themselves with people smarter than them, but they also look for talent and innovation throughout their organisation. A great example of this is a CEO who recognises he needs help with technology and relating to younger members of his business — therefore he finds himself a reverse mentor (someone younger) who's been in the business for a far shorter time who can help him understand and relate to the "Gen Z" and how they can best succeed together.

Sharing Mistakes as well as Successes

Leaders don't hide their mistakes. Great leaders understand that by demonstrating some vulnerability and admitting errors that they've made and how they learnt from them, can inspire others — especially other potential leaders. When a leader is accountable and owns their mistakes, this actually increases people's trust in them. Think about the opposite approach: imagine a leader who fudges and twists their words in an attempt to reframe or deflect from the truth, therefore avoiding responsibility or a leader who blames someone else entirely. These behaviours and attitudes erode and eventually demolish trust as people see through the false narratives.

Leaders also need to know what transparency isn't. Transparency isn't oversharing. It's not exposing all your thoughts, worries, fears, "what ifs" and "maybes" in an unfiltered, uncontrolled dump. Leaders still have a responsibility to manage their own emotions and regulate themselves. Transparency is clear about knowns and unknowns; emotions may be involved in a thoughtful and authentic way that connects a leader to their people. This promotes a sense of confidence even in uncertain and difficult situations.

Where Do we Go from Here?

If you're feeling like this is too much of a minefield to navigate, the good news is that being transparent is a leadership skill we can practice and master. There are some very simple, straight-forward ways to increase transparency (and therefore trust) within your organisation. It's all about communication.

Why not start by simply increasing the volume of communication? Internal comms are crucial and when done well they aren't just to share information, but to help people feel connected and foster a sense of belonging. Studies suggest that we take in between twenty-five and fifty percent of what we hear — that isn't very much. Add in a stress factor (perhaps it's bad news, perhaps an individual has other concerns fighting for the attention), then you can be sure that the percentage will reduce even further. Don't be afraid to repeat the message. In fact, you need to expect to repeat it more than once.

Let's not forget that we're all different, so not only do we need to consider how much and how often we communicate but *how* we communicate. We need to use a variety of methods, including in-person meetings where possible: emails, slides with visuals and so on. We need to make sure all the facts, rationale and vision are included too.

Communicate in a timely manner. Don't hold back information unnecessarily — there'll always be the risk that people will hear via a leak or external source and then our people will likely attribute all sorts of unhelpful reasons as to why we withheld the information. Suspicion and distrust will almost certainly follow. So even if we don't have all the information, let's be honest about it and update as soon as possible.

Let's remember that we're all on a journey to learn and practice improving our skills and making small changes. Sticking to such principles is always the best way to achieve sustainable growth. As you reflect on your transparency skills, pick one thing to start doing or do differently. As Indira Gandhi is reported to have said, "Have a bias toward action. Let's see something happen now. You can break that big plan into small steps and take the first step right away." Don't wait — decide now and act!

Relatability is about showing people that they can trust your heart.

Chapter 7
Trustworthy Leaders
Relate Well

Finding Common Ground

We've all been there, haven't we?

In those moments where we chunter away to ourselves.

This job would be perfect, if it wasn't for the students, thinks the exasperated teacher who's repeatedly been sworn at all week.

Life would be so much easier without the patients, mutters the nurse under his breath as he walks away with bite marks all the way up his arm.

If only I didn't have to deal with customers, the frustrated store manager vents, as yet another belligerent exchange takes place.

If it wasn't for the parishioners, this job would be a joy, the deflated vicar ponders while staring in disbelief at the three-sided email of complaints (not to be taken personally of course!).

Life would be so much better without people, wouldn't it? Or maybe that needs rephrasing, without *some* people!

But as John Andrew Holmes once wrote, "It's well to remember that the entire universe, with one trifling exception, is composed of others."

And the "others" that it's composed of, contains the "some."

People can bring out the best and worst in us. And inevitably that means that *we* can bring out the best or worst in others. As leaders we're to be ever looking for and creating opportunities to allow our people the space to thrive, flourish and excel. Where will we see this happening? In high trust environments: high trust environments that we've cultivated.

To demonstrate that we can be trusted and will in turn trust, we need to practice the art of relatability, even with the "some."

Yes, there are people in life we feel we will just never connect with. We ask ourselves, where is the "common ground?" And swiftly conclude that there is none.

But is this an accurate assessment?

Surely there's always something in common to be found between ourselves and the fellow citizens we share the planet with. After all, we have to conclude that we're all human beings, even though that may need quite some convincing! So, let's start there. Humanity is always our common ground. Whilst personalities, interests, hobbies, values, experiences and so on may be wildly different, the essence of what makes us human is the same. We'll all love, laugh, feel pain and disappointment, have hopes and dreams, and sadly but undeniably have an opinion on the weather.

The human race is beautifully amazing and wonderfully strange all at the same time and we as leaders get to experience this every day. Even in those moments when we don't think any commonality can be found, we need to realise that it can and it's our responsibility as the leader to be the one that finds it, nurtures it and appreciates it.

Leadership involves people which in turn requires relationships. But not just any relationships. It's good, solid, healthy relationships that create productivity and help a business or organisation to flourish, and relatability sits at the heart. John Maxwell rightly observed that "in trying to relate to others, many leaders forget to be relatable."

When we're relatable, other people are able to bond or associate with us because they perceive a "common ground" and this fosters a greater level of trust between the leader and her people. Relatability however isn't to be mistaken with likability. Being relatable is about interacting with a person on an individual basis and demonstrating that there is a reason for us to connect with them, subsequently allowing them to connect with us.

The relatable leader is authentically himself/herself and values others for being authentically themselves.

Relatability Sells and Wins

Relatability in the world of marketing, was the buzzword of 2020. Companies were being awakened to the need to make their brand relatable to the customer. This is why reflecting on the advertising over Christmas 2020, so many of the big retail stores marketed their brand by empathising with the nation's frustrations and sadness in the grips of the global pandemic. The emphasis was on home and the family, giving to community causes and encouraging us all to share the love throughout our neighbourhoods.

Relatability is powerful. Relatability sells.

This is realised brilliantly when it comes to public speaking engagements. How many presentations have we all sat through in our lives? I'm guessing enough for us all to know what makes for a really amazing, knock-you-off-your-chair type of presentation and what makes for a pretty dull, tiresome and mediocre one. There are several ingredients that we could list, however a special one in particular would have to be the art of connecting with your audience. There's nothing quite like that feeling of walking away from a speech by someone who has oozed relatability: you feel you know the person speaking and they know you. Such a connection inspires instant buy-in, automatic allegiance and long-term loyal followers. It's a winning strategy, demonstrated throughout political and presidential campaigns the world over. People vote for a leader who connects.

And in the same way relatability will win with your people.

The Heart Matters

Whereas many of the other trust-building skills are about getting people to trust your mind, relatability is about showing people that they can trust your heart. It shows empathy and understanding, care and concern. It's this that produces loyalty, where performance is enhanced, productivity increased and people enthused.

Strong connections between a leader and her people mean that there's more of a willingness to go the extra mile, to help, to support and to align themselves with her vision. They don't just trust in her ability and skill, they're now able to trust in her motives as well.

As leaders we're experts at getting fixated on strategy and vision, marketing and growth and a range of all other vitally important factors. But we overlook the individual at great cost to all these things: The expansion of our business and the growth of our organisation depends on individuals.

It's up to Us not Them

Many leaders due to their position, can be mistaken in thinking that it's not their responsibility to connect and be relatable. Rather, it's the responsibility of the other. This couldn't be further from the truth. Leaders must lead by example. We must be the first to demonstrate and model that which we want to nurture and develop.

If you want your people to have your back, you must first have theirs. If you want your people to value you and their role in the organisation, then they need to know they're valued.

The boss who continues to refer to the young employee as "the girl" fails to see their own self-sabotage. Why would she want to work hard for such a person? Why should she give of her best for this leader? She may well do her "job" because she's being paid, but to really give her all, there's no reason. We as leaders must give our people the reasons for them to work at their natural best.

Pay, position, bonuses — while all are motivating factors and of absolute necessity — will only go so far in producing productivity. The reward of being respected, valued, listened to, cared for and understood have the potential to reap far greater benefits — with little or no financial cost. Emotional intelligence, which incorporates the ability to not only know one's own emotions, but to recognise and influence the emotions of others, is vastly underrated as a leadership skill.

Where are We on the Relatability Scale?

Relatability comes far more easily for some than others. Some of us are more naturally inclined to take the time to listen and show an interest in others — we enjoy it and it's not hard work. However, for others, we'll have to make a conscious, concerted effort to do so. Is this not the way with so many things though? But whether it comes naturally or not, we all have the responsibility to put relatability high on the agenda if we're to create high trust.

One of the greatest sayings of all time, is the golden rule, "Treat others as you want to be treated." When it comes to relatability, perhaps what we really need to be thinking is "Treat others as they want to be treated." And how do our people want to be treated? Do we know? They're all individuals who are unique in personality, preferences and talents. Keep asking questions and choose to be interested in people and what matters to them. Do we know our team members; their unique challenges and goals? Do we support them and challenge them in a tailored way? Communication is key to relatability. Keep communication frequent. Have regular conversations with people and actually schedule those conversations in the diary; don't just leave it to chance.

We need to ask ourselves the continual question: How are we doing on the relatability scale? How are we helping people to know us and at the same time making people feel known by us? Do we show our own vulnerability and are we honest with people? We need to show that we're not infallible and we can do this by sharing a story now and again about our own personal struggle or mistakes made. Not oversharing but sharing within reason can go a long way in building strong and healthy relationships.

Do we take an interest in others? Do we listen and listen well; paying attention to what is actually being said and precede to act on what we hear? Listening goes far beyond hearing. We need to listen with our whole selves. There's nothing worse than having a conversation with someone who's looking over your shoulder, distracted by something else. To give our full attention and then take the relevant action that's needed if necessary from what we've heard, contributes to a trusting environment.

The new CEO of a large organisation made their first goal to remember each person's name. That may not sound too hard, but when you have hundreds of people working alongside you and have little direct contact, this is quite a task. But an extremely worthwhile one. We need to be creative with relatability, especially if we do indeed lead an organisation where hundreds of people work, or hundreds of people attend. Relatability starts with us and we model it then to our close team of leaders and the people in the organisation we do know, so that they in turn lead with relatability towards their teams. We can be relatable and relate to others in many ways: it's creating a culture of relatability that is paramount, but we're the catalyst.

When we're relatable to our people, we'll experience within them an increased level of confidence where they're more inclined to explore new things and take greater risks. This is because they'll trust that we care, that we understand and that we're cheering them on. Trust is forged in the moments of connection: we must be the ones to ensure that those connections take place. The trustworthy leader is relatable.

THE LEADERS BOOK

Consistency is all about the cumulative effect. It's the art of doing little things day in and day out that over time will amount in the big thing: trust!

Chapter 8
Trustworthy Leaders
Walk the Walk

Where's the Allure?

The consistent leader! This is hardly the title for a new bestseller. One may ask oneself, where the allure is. Why is it we tend to perceive the ideas of consistency, predictability and steadiness as a little underwhelming? The dynamic leader, the inspirational leader and the courageous leader all sound a tad more exciting. However, we all know that at the heart of good, healthy leadership has to be the principle of consistency; *no* consistency is a lot *less* alluring in the long run. The dynamism, inspiration and courage of the aforementioned leader are weakened without the constancy and predictability of consistency. The inconsistent leader will never achieve the high trust environment that they aspire to create, however dynamic, inspirational and courageous they are. Emboldening our people to trust us, lies with our ability to be consistent. Consistent behaviour, words and action have to be demonstrated for trust to be fostered.

Of course, there's always the possibility that a leader *will be* consistent, but consistently awful: the leader who prides themselves in being consistently successful but by ill-gotten means isn't the consistency we're looking for! To be consistent is to act or do things over time, in a constantly fair and accurate way. If society is deemed to have a trust crisis today, then the answer isn't simply to build more trust, but become more trustable. We shouldn't tell our people to just blindly trust us, but we need to demonstrate that we're trustworthy — able to be trusted. Consistency (doing the right, fair and accurate thing) births this quality. We can't afford to dismiss consistency. If we do, it'll cost us greatly.

People want consistency.

Some years ago, Colgate launched a new consumer range: the Colgate Kitchen Entrees. Who'd have ever thought that we would read Colgate and kitchen together? But that's indeed what happened. In an attempt to further its brand, Colgate turned their hand to frozen ready meals. But the customer was having none of it. It just didn't add up for people. Colgate was all about the minty fresh breath, not a ready-meal delicacy. It was far too confusing. And suffice to say, the Colgate Kitchen Entrees, quickly became a thing of the past. Just like customers want brand consistency, our people want leadership consistency. Anything else isn't just confusing, but when it comes to leadership, quite frankly, disrespectful.

Keep it on Repeat!

Because consistency demands that we continue to do the right things over time, it's therefore, not good enough for us as leaders to only meet our commitments sometimes — whether that's being punctual for meetings, keeping appointments, showing support and understanding or staying true to our promises to name but a few examples. Rather we need to *always* do these things. It's this that creates the trust that we want to develop in our people.

We sometimes mistakenly think that it's the big one-off gestures that really matter. We may deliver on the promised promotion and feel justified that this will be enough for our employee to trust us. But if we fail to deliver on the promise of having a conversation, getting them assistance or help and not allowing flexible working hours that were agreed upon (or any other number of things), then we lose credibility and damage trust.

Consistency is all about the cumulative effect. It's the art of doing little things day in and day out that over time will amount in the big thing: trust! Would you trust the employee who turns up to a meeting on time once to always turn up on time? Well, possibly, but not likely. You'll more readily trust them when they continually turn up on time and show themselves trustable.

You're not an Exception to the Rule!

As Immanuel Kant famously postulated in the idea of the categorical imperative, we can't be an exception to the rule, "Act only according to that maxim by which you can at the same time will that it should become a universal law." As leaders we must set the example and we must act in the way we want our people to act. There's to be no distinction; we don't have immunity because we're the leader. The teacher who's trying to instil fairness, equality and respect will have a hard time justifying why jumping ahead at the dinner queue is acceptable.

The principle "do as I say; not as I do" can all too often manifest itself within the life of a leader. We only have to look at the world's leading politicians in the lockdown of 2020/21. The public outcry was fervent, as stories of politicians breaking lockdown rules began to emerge. We ask ourselves why would they risk it and put their reputation and position in such jeopardy? But perhaps it's that exact position that made way for the rule breaking — the belief that their position would mean they were protected and the thought that somehow their position elevated them to a different level. Sounds absurd, doesn't? However, as leaders of any type of organisation we're in danger of falling into that same way of thinking. A "doing-things-that-I-say-not-to-do" mentality will only serve to damage our credibility and reputation.

It's important for us to consider the type of mindset that we're adopting as it will indeed affect the organisation's overall culture. If we believe it's one rule for us and one rule for them and we can be as inconsistent as we like, then we shouldn't be surprised if this filters down through the organisation. The expectations of our people need to be aligned to the expectation we have of ourselves.

Yo-Yo Leadership

When our behaviours, actions and moods as leaders reflects a yo-yo — up-and-down style — we result in creating an environment of uncertainty. One of the greatest factors to developing a high performing team is to ensure psychological safety for all. This involves a safe space where team members can take risks and be vulnerable; confident that they won't be embarrassed or punished for their mistakes. If there's no certainty to a leader's behaviour, it becomes impossible for a psychological safe environment to be maintained. An erratic leadership style harnesses no stability and this in turn can cause stress, fear and disengagement in our teams.

This can also be said for our decision-making as leaders as well. If we're inconsistent with our decisions, flip-flopping between one course of action and another, changing our minds etc.; then this will breed uncertainty, frustration and fatigue. This doesn't mean we can't change our decisions. Wisdom and courage can often dictate that we should. However it's about being consistent in how we manage that. Rather than just announce the change, we should ensure that all in the original decision-making process have been consulted and we reconnect with them and communicate clearly our thoughts.

Vision and Values

One of the top priorities when considering how consistency affords stability and security, is with regards to our vision and values. Our decisions and behaviours categorically must adhere to the vision of our organisation and the values to which it holds to. Values mean absolutely nothing unless they're actioned. Many companies, schools and religious organisations will proudly state their values from the platform — the glossy magazines and painted walls. However, all credibility and trust is lost if these aren't upheld.

How are the vision and values of your organisation informing your choices, culture, strategy and day-to-day decisions? Visions and values aren't to be spoken about once a year on a particular "vision day" or at a "vision meeting." They're the foundation and the heart of any organisation. Every time you meet, begin the meeting with them. When you give feedback to people, use them and when you're considering future ventures or investments questions, ask yourself whether they align with them. You get the point? Be consistent: eat and sleep your vision and values!

No Favourites

It's a tricky one this one, isn't it? Because — let's face it — we all have favourites. In every sphere of life we have favourites: whether it be a favourite restaurant, holiday destination or quality street chocolate. There's no escaping it. And when it comes to people; well, it's even more so. But part of what it means to be a consistent leader is to ensure that we treat people fairly, equally and equitably. A great leader should avoid partiality. Whilst it would be naive to ever think we'd like everybody to the same degree, we must ensure that we don't allow this to cloud our judgement or actions. We must be consistent with all people and to all people: there's no place for favouritism that leads to inconsistencies in our leadership.

As a former schoolteacher, the one thing that would really annoy students would be inconsistency from teachers with regards to homework deadlines. There's nothing more soul-destroying and infuriating for the diligent student who had worked hard to get their homework in on time, to watch the student who hadn't, get a reprieve. Now, as a teacher (and one who was trying hard to always be fair), reprieves were sometimes extremely necessary. However, to let the student off who had no good reason and who simply couldn't be bothered or was absent-minded, was a bridge too far! Consistency means that we're clear on our expectations and we hold to them — for everyone. There can't be different treatment for different people.

In it for the Long Game

Sometimes we might think that success, growth and productivity come from the big things — the spectacular. But actually, often they come from the small things and the day-in-day-out consistent behaviours and actions that we continue to display. In the world we live in today, where everything is happening so quickly and patience seems to have fallen out of fashion, to put time and effort into building trust can seem like too much hard work. But to build trust we have to be in the long game. There are no easy shortcuts. Leadership is all about consistency. Trust is forged when people see a leader truly walk the walk.

Blind optimism that denies the difficulties is dangerous.

Chapter 9
Trustworthy Leaders
Exercise Good Judgement

Excellent leaders possess wisdom. They might be described as intuitive, well informed — perhaps even shrewd. This type of wisdom is closely associated with the idea of feasibility: exercising good judgement and the ability to evaluate a scenario and chart a stretching (yet possible) path forward. This is essential if our people are to trust us.

Big dreams can inspire people, but if a leader fails to deliver, people will be less enthusiastic about backing the next big idea. A string of overpromises will result in outright scepticism and inertia. In contrast, sound, effective, thoughtful planning combined with big dreams create a potent environment for any team; sparking energy and propelling action.

Real Faith isn't Blind

Without doubt, a healthy dose of optimism is a helpful attribute for any leader. After all, if you don't believe that things will improve in the future, why would anyone else? Creating belief and pointing your people towards a better future to engage them in the necessary tasks is essential. Accepting the harsh facts of reality is equally critical. In essence, this is what feasibility is about; the ability to maintain an unwavering faith in the eventual outcome whilst at the same time accepting the hard facts of reality.

Some leaders we encounter draw on excessive charisma to motivate their people. This can work well initially: we can all be roused by an energetic speech, an appeal to a brighter future and promises of success and glory. This will be short-lived if the leader ignores the difficult facts and realities. Dismissing evidence that doesn't fit the desired narrative creates the conditions for failure; both in performance and morale. Eventually the realities will be seen — "Look, the emperor has no clothes on!" — and the leader's credibility is destroyed.

Other leaders are excessively cautious, seeking to identify every potential problem and difficulty before taking any action. Exaggerated caution is no less damaging.

Buses. We hear a lot about buses when working with leaders. Whether people are on them or off them or being thrown under them! Feasibility is checking the basics before getting on the bus: it has four wheels (at least), sufficient fuel and enough seats. When heading to its destination, the driver is aware of their dashboard, the driving conditions and how their passengers are feeling. Here's the crucial part: they adapt accordingly. They have their eyes open. Have you ever been on a bus where the driver is blindfolded? No, I thought not (you're alive and reading this!).

Real faith, open-eyes faith, is hard work. We have dreams and visions for the future and then something difficult, possibly devastating, crops up. We hear of a personal failure in one of our trusted team members. We hear on the grapevine that a major customer is looking at alternative providers. We're alerted by our safety team that one of our oil rigs is dangerous. Mostly, we don't want to hear these things. We can excuse them away — "Jamal is just stressed; he'll get over it," "The customer won't leave us; our competitor is rubbish," and "The rig won't blow; it's gotten through worse conditions than these." Wise leaders choose to open their eyes and ears and act. They investigate, reprioritise their schedule and allocate resources to gathering information (quickly) — adapting their plans if needed. They don't deny the truth and at the same time they don't lose sight of the eventual, compelling objective.

Weak leaders dismiss the bad news as fake news; blustering forward and removing those people who bring the difficult realities to light. Weak leaders tend to ignore the warnings.

Blind optimism that denies the difficulties is dangerous.

What's Worked Before won't Necessarily Work Again

Thinking back to my childhood, I remember my dad asking the same question of the check-out staff every time we went out to buy an electrical item: "Can I have a free plug please?" As bizarre as it might seem to some people reading this, electrical goods didn't come with a fitted plug — just the exposed cables. Between 1980 and 1988, 32 people died and 3,000 were hospitalised due to faulty DIY plug-fitting. It was only in 1992 that fitted plugs became compulsory.

Change happens all the time. And yet, we can too easily revert to what's worked in the past when considering our current and future challenges and fail to see the risks in repeating former strategies.

It's understandable. We invest significant effort and energy in solving problems early in our careers and in the early stages of building a company. We throw ourselves at the issues with blood, sweat and tears. When our strategies work out, we're set up to repeat them rather than go through the pain all over again. That's a good thing; it's efficient. Until we become too quick to rely on past approaches and apply them uncritically. Even a great advisor today might not be the person you need for tomorrow's issues.

Feasibility includes challenging conventional ideas: "Is this still the best strategy?" "Is she still the best person to guide us for the next three years?" "Is our product meeting the needs of future customers?" Evidenced answers are sought and embraced, despite the effort and resources that it'll take to change direction.

There are a number of global trends that demand all of us to face up to our conventional thinking. If your response to any of the following is that it doesn't matter to you, take that as a warning signal that this might be the very thing you need to choose to focus on:

- A digitised world. Digital technology is transforming our world. We can buy and sell practically anything almost instantly. We can communicate immediately to a global audience. Artificial Intelligence (AI) enables us to create art, currency, businesses and even relationships. Organisations that cling to old systems and deny the need to continually digitise, will struggle to survive. A small example: It astounds me that some companies still have a fax number.

- Ways of working. The way people want to work, especially in traditional office work, has fundamentally changed. Flexibility is no longer a differentiator — it's standard. Broadly stated, expectations for career success are different too. The idea of a job for life — even a vocation for life — is strange to the emerging workforce. Many expect to achieve higher status roles in ever-shorter timeframes and with less blood, sweat and tears than former generations would have expected. This is neither good nor bad, but it's certainly different.

- Environmental and social impact. Climate change is happening and will impact all of us in some way. "Hundred year" weather events are now more like "once a decade" events. As with all change, there may be opportunities but only for those willing to challenge their conventional thinking. Social impact — how our organisations are helping or hurting other people — is also increasingly important for stakeholders (employees and customers especially).

Check Your Bias

Everyone is biased. It's the way humans are wired. Our brains are masters at energy efficiency; creating automatic, unconscious actions. Like breathing. We hardly ever think about breathing, it's something that just happens automatically, without us having to think of taking every breath (thankfully). If we don't breathe, we die.

In its quest for efficiency, our brains can create fast connections that are not always quite as true as we would like to believe. These are our biases. For example, we can be naturally biased towards people with similar experiences as us; they lived in the same town, or went to the same university, have a similar family upbringing, enjoy the same sorts of things. This is called affinity bias. And it's unconscious.

There are many types of bias. These unconscious fast choices are creating beliefs and actions that may be true sometimes but are not as permanently true as we think. If you're not sure what your biases might be, you could take the Harvard Implicit Association Test. I was initially surprised to discover my own strong bias towards a particular type of person, yet on reflection I know that the test has correctly identified a bias. You could ask trusted friends and colleagues to tell you honestly what they think your biases are. Once we are aware - conscious - of our biases, we can choose to challenge our instinctive choices and make better informed decisions.

Our sunk-cost bias is one that will compromise feasibility. This is our tendency to continue with a course of action because of the money and time that's already gone into it, even when fresh evaluation tells us that we should cut our losses and redeploy our remaining resources elsewhere. Consider recruiting. There are very few good reasons to extend a new joiner's probationary period. After all, if after 3 months (sometimes longer) it's not working out well, we have all the information we need. Yet we can be biased towards extending probation or passing someone who, deep down, we know isn't right for us. Why? We've invested money and time recruiting them in a tight employment market. The right choice is to let them go and restart the recruitment process. The easy choice is to pass them, and hope things change (they rarely do).

The same goes for investments in technology, equipment, marketing plans, product lines - anything strategic. We want these decisions to work out, so we look for reasons to continue rather than embrace new information that shows they are not.

Leaders with feasibility skill check their biases. They seek to become aware of them and continually evaluate, understand when the easy choice is not the right choice and act accordingly.

Evaluate Resources

According to research by CB Insights, running out of cash is the main reason that start-ups fail, accounting for 38% of all failures. Whilst there are a number of reasons for excessive cash burn, poor judgement is certainly one of them. Stretching expectations can be healthy and compelling. Utterly unrealistic ideals can be blinding and destructive. There's a tension here. Good leadership includes imagination, dreaming and engaging the heart. Not being constrained by over-caution, nor focussing solely on what's immediately apparent. Yet too much imagination and too little analysis will set the conditions for unfeasible expectations - and failure.

Leaders who possess feasibility skill will evaluate their resources when setting a course of action. They regularly re-evaluate to critically assess whether capacity is expanding or contracting. Resources in scope are not limited to financial metrics or the number of employees. It includes morale in the organisation, personal energy, willingness of supporters to help and access to networks. A leader adept at practicing feasibility skill is not so much cautious as opportunistic. This is less about counting the beans and more about identifying where beans might be found, but without engaging in baseless fantasies.

Counting what we have is the business of the manager.

Using resources to create new opportunities is the enterprise of the leader.

Making things appear out of thin air is the trick of the magician.

We can explore this idea further by considering some common sayings:

- "Go big or go home." Ambitious dreams and objectives are fundamental to achieving change. Objectives that are too big, however, will more often result in going home. Swimming the Channel sounds like a "go big" event to me. Without experience and training, attempting this feat would be unrealistic and dangerous. The principle is the same in our organisations.

- "Rome wasn't built in a day." Setting ourselves timeframes are important to help focus our efforts. However, when deadlines are unreasonable and become an end in themselves, we run the risk of breaking ourselves, our people and possibly even our organisations to try to hit them. They are called deadlines for a reason! We are more in charge of our timeframes than we think. If more time is required to complete a project, then reassess and give it more time. That doesn't mean the idea is dead, it means that we need to give it more time.

- "Jam tomorrow". This phrase is from Lewis Carroll's classic book "Through the Looking Glass and What Alice Found There". In an interaction with the White Queen, Alice is promised "jam tomorrow and jam yesterday, but never jam today." The phrase has come to mean that promises are constantly unfulfilled, especially where the goalposts frequently shift. "We'll get there tomorrow" but tomorrow never arrives. In contrast, proper consideration of the resources ensures that promises are realistic and more likely to be achieved.

Without good judgement, our people won't trust us, at least not consistently. What will help you to elevate your judgement? Here are some prompts that may help you:

- Are you listening to the right data? Can you include non-financial metrics in your analysis? Complicated dashboards can be confusing, reports designed years ago may no longer provide you with the data you really need.

- Are you receiving input from unusual sources both within and outside of your organisation? Sometimes the people whose company you don't enjoy much have the perspectives that will help you see the realities.

- Do you listen with an open mind or an open mouth? Listen to learn, to understand; be interested and curious. Ask clarifying questions. Resist the urge to listen with the sole aim of defending your position.

Exercising good judgement and acting wisely is essential if we are to be worthy of our people's trust.

THE LEADERS BOOK

Power itself is neither good nor bad, it is how a leader uses their power that matters.

Chapter 10
Trustworthy Leaders
Share Power

Empowerment allows people to trust themselves whilst at the same time increasing trust in the leader.

But empowerment is probably one of the most overused and under practised words in the world of work. Many people are confused about what it actually is and how to achieve it, some dismiss it as merely a buzzword and throwback to the late 20th century, some misunderstand or even manipulate empowerment for their own gain, others still lose hope of ever achieving real empowerment or put it in the "too difficult to deal with box". Leaders also often miss the vital connection between empowerment and trust.

Let's start at the beginning, clarifying what empowerment is and isn't.

Empowerment is "the act or action of empowering someone or something: the granting of the power, right, or authority to perform various acts or duties". Now as a definition this seems very clear and concise, as a definition should be. But we need to look a little closer to begin to understand some of the complexities, confusion and resistance to truly creating an empowering workplace and truly empowering your people.

Power

Power. Yes, we need to have the conversation about power. What thought popped into your head? Or what did you feel when you read the word power? Did you feel uncomfortable with the word? What judgement did you make? Do you instinctively view power as good or bad? Power in and of itself is neither inherently good or bad, but we often err on the negative view perhaps because or negative experiences where leaders have misused power and there are many of those in our world. And it's also likely we are familiar with the well-known phrase "power corrupts, absolute power corrupts absolutely" a phrase written by a British politician, Lord Acton in 1887, in a letter addressing a very specific issue, and arguably taken out of context.

We would prefer Voltaire's quote on power, made popular through Marvel's Spider-man, "With great power, comes great responsibility." The person who holds power (great or not) has a responsibility to use it wisely, with integrity and moral courage. And whatever you think or feel about power, as leaders we have it, so we must learn how best to use it and, hopefully, commit to use it for a greater purpose than ourselves. Power itself is neither good nor bad, it is how a leader uses their power that matters. We have a responsibility to lead ourselves and our people well, power is fundamental in making any changes, and we need to be aware of how others perceive the power that we have and how we use it. We are negligent if we say we do not have power and refuse to recognise the impact we as leaders have on others around us precisely because we do have power. Recognising our power and the influence it gives us does not need to be arrogant, we can, and we recommend, should, be humble about the power and position we are in as leaders. Being humble means that we recognise the talents, skills and gifts that we possess but we are not self-promoting, our ego is in check and we also recognise and value other people's talent too, without feeling inferior.

Going back to the definition of empowerment, essentially leaders grant people the power to carry out certain duties, and certain roles. Empowerment can only happen where there is already a power imbalance. As leaders we have to choose to share the power that we have; work out how we do that; with whom we share; and when we do it. But firstly. . .why would we choose to share in the first place?

Empowering others, sharing the power in the organisation, can have a great number of benefits, and there are a number of cautions to consider too. So to quote Simon Sinek "Start with your why". This may sound obvious but if you are not clear about why you are choosing to empower your people and make empowerment central to the culture of your organisation you will likely give up at the first difficulty - and there will be difficulties.

We believe that people are the most important part of any organisation, and if you commit to growing people, they will likely commit to grow the business, the charity, the organisation. Leaders could think of themselves like farmers or gardeners, creating the right conditions for healthy growth and flourishing. Healthy growth needs attention, time and a long-term perspective, it doesn't happen quickly (unless we're talking about weeds, but that is a whole other chapter!) Empowering people stretches them, challenges them and grows them. When people feel genuinely empowered, they feel much more engaged in the workplace, they are much more productive, they perform better, they are happier and healthier and they contribute to that important, positive, healthy work culture.

Choosing to share your power also releases you to focus on the areas that you need to, for example, the vision, the dream even, seeing the bigger picture clearly, understanding your organisation more deeply and developing yourself and your leadership. You will also be able to spot the talent in your organisation and therefore make good investments and plan well for your succession - the business has to thrive beyond your tenure, none of us are indispensable.

There are some essential ingredients that we need to implement well in order to successfully empower others and build trust:

Clear communication is a must - people need to be very clear about the task we are empowering them to do, and they need to be clear about our expectations otherwise we will both resent the experience and be unlikely to repeat it. It would also help them to understand why we have asked them, what have we seen in them that we want to nurture and grow.

Choose well - we need to remember why we are doing this, is it just to off load a task (that's not really empowerment by the way!) or are we looking for the growth of our people and organisation? Hopefully the latter, in which case we need to empower people who we have observed have the necessary attitude, skills and abilities, or the potential skills and abilities, to achieve what we are asking, with support. We want to encourage and stretch people, not set them unreasonable and unattainable goals. Let's be clear, this does not mean we empower some and not others, but we may want to consider how we empower individuals, we need to know our people - what excites and energises them? What are they passionate about? What are their long-term aspirations? Which ones align with organisational plans and values?

Support – empowerment isn't a dump and run exercise. We need to set people up well and we need to check in regularly (without micromanaging) to see how they are progressing and if they have the resources they need to achieve the desired outcome. Just as we have emphasised the need to be clear about the task, leaders need to be clear about the support that is provided too.

Give people permission to fail – DO NOT leave this ingredient out! Failure is a very natural, normal part of growth. Sir James Dyson reportedly went through five thousand one hundred and twenty-six vacuum designs before he produced a working vacuum, it took Thomas Edison over one thousand attempts before he successfully created the light bulb; learning a sport or musical instrument, it all takes practice, patience and perseverance. The most important attitude we need to have in empowering others is allowing them to fail, and fail well, which means we must learn from it. Henry Ford has been quoted as saying "Failure is simply the opportunity to begin again, this time more intelligently." To be clear, this is not the same as promoting or allowing recklessness or negligence, but rather creating the environment where people are not afraid to explore different approaches, try new ideas in the full knowledge they may not be perfect.

If any of this sounds too hard or too risky, then we need to consider the impact of not empowering our people. Whilst it may be possible to run a successful business or organisation without empowering others, it will surely die when that leader leaves, or re-invention will be inevitable.

Let's spend a few moments considering. . .if we are not empowering people:

- We will lose the best talent we have, probably to competitors.
- We will miss out on so many ideas to improve the efficiency and effectiveness of the organisation.
- We will suck the joy, energy and creativity out of the organisation.
- We will be forcing ourselves to work longer and harder than we need to.
- We will miss out on family time as a result.
- We will struggle to recruit talent.

Sharing Power Well

There are a number of examples of how well Southwest Airlines empower their staff. A number of years ago, after the airline company had rebranded, it was clear their uniforms needed a complete refresh too. An easy and common option would have been to hire an external company to design them. However, Southwest Airlines turned instead to their employees. They invited anyone interested in helping to design the new uniforms to come forward, and when so many did they had to whittle numbers down to a task force of forty three. This group met every two weeks, over a period of nineteen months, to collaborate on the new design. The result was a uniform that employees genuinely liked, were proud to wear and were practical and easy to maintain - they were made of machine washable materials, a rarity in the airline industry.

A cynic might say that the airline was going for the cheap option, cheaper than hiring a company. But that's just not true. Southwest Airlines have a well-established reputation for empowering employees - take the baggage handler who plays his ukulele to customers when he has a spare moment, because who wouldn't smile in that moment? Southwest Airlines also had to commit to release over forty employees to work on this additional project over a substantial time frame, with no guarantees what the outcome would be. Southwest Airlines trusted their employees with their brand, and their image - and the risk paid off, not only in the completion of the task, but another example of their positive company reputation.

Take a Look in the Mirror!

If you are a leader struggling to empower your people and the above rationale does nothing to move you to action, we may need to take a deeper look at what's happening, there may be an ugly truth at the root of these struggles. One of the greatest barriers to empowerment for a leader is pride. Yes, it's true that pride is not always negative, it's great that we take pride in our work, it's great that we want to strive for excellence, and do well in our chosen career, in these examples pride shows that we care about what we do and take care of what we have.

Pride becomes a real danger when it tips over into arrogance and becomes egocentric. When we believe that no-one can do it better, that we are always right, that we have all the best ideas, we are disempowering others, deceiving ourselves and neglecting our organisation. Pride like this will stop us truly partnering or collaborating and will certainly prevent us from empowering others, because we will want to take the credit but not the responsibility for mistakes, and glory hunting may become our only goal. Destructive pride can also be more subtle. It might become evident when we find ourselves not able to ask for help when we need it, always needing affirmation, bringing the attention back to ourselves, disregarding advice from others or even seeing certain tasks as below us.

So, take a deep breath. . .could pride be a barrier stopping us from becoming great leaders? The good news is that once you have identified the issue you can work the problem. If pride is getting in your way you can choose to behave with humility instead.

Practice gratitude. Notice and appreciate others, thank them and be specific.

- Ask for ideas and input on a project and truly consider those contributions.
- Ask for feedback, start with people you trust to tell you the truth, not just what they think you want to hear.
- Celebrate and share successes with your team.
- Make a list of all the talent in your organisation and identify ways to grow that talent.
- Get a coach or a mentor.

Be encouraged

Learning to truly empower those around you may be one of the most rewarding skills you can learn, even if you have to get out of your own way to do it. Authentic trust relies on the sharing of power.

THE LEADERS BOOK

Living Legacy

leaders will need to steer their organisations to become architects of a new economy - one which is optimised for human wellbeing and planetary health - rather than one optimised purely for financial maximisation, regardless of the impact on humans and the planet.

Leaders today must not only navigate the future, they must consciously build it. Decisions made today will have significant consequences for many generations to come. That is both an enormous responsibility and an incredible opportunity for a truly meaningful use of one's working life. There is no precedent for this kind of paradigm shift on the scale of a global economy. There are no experts who have done this before, there is no "best practice" to learn from, no case studies to pore over. The pace of change is extraordinary, the consequences are potentially existential.

If the past is no longer a useful predictor of the future, what will guide their choices? How can this generation of leaders make decisions wisely, knowing the impacts of those decisions will be felt by all their current stakeholders (employees, customers, suppliers, investors, regulators, the environment, society as a whole)... and future ones too?

During times of extraordinary change, it can be useful to focus on the fundamentals that hold true in all circumstances - but that can be easily forgotten or lost in the chaos, complexity and confusion that are all features of change. The role of a leader of an organisation of any size is to create space and time to think through, and support others to think through, the answers to some fundamental questions. For instance:

- What is important to me as a human being? How would I wish to reflect on my life when I look back - on my work, my relationships, my sense of purpose?

- Why have we come together as a group of people in an organisation? What are we trying to achieve collectively? How does that help meet the needs of people and planet?

- How do we think about people? Do we see them as individual human beings with inherent dignity, or as assets or resources that can be used instrumentally? Does the quality of our relationships internally and externally matter to us? How does that show up?

- How do we hold ourselves accountable for all the impacts we have - positive and negative? Do we invite public scrutiny and engage with critics?

The leaders of this generation will play a defining role in shaping the future of people and planet. The impacts of their decisions will be evident in their own lifetimes, those of their children and beyond. As a leader at this point in history, it is worth spending time thinking deeply about the legacy you aspire to leave.

> *Yet without a cause, a core belief, it is difficult - extremely difficult - to lead with excellence, inspire others to meaningful action and create a truly living legacy.*

Chapter 11
Legacy-Minded Leaders
Prioritise Purpose

The best leaders exude a strong sense of purpose. Purpose underpins a living legacy. A living legacy is one that influences the lives of other people now in the present; in our work, families and communities.

"What is the point of this?" I found myself asking this question about most meetings, board reports and investment analysis work I was doing, whilst volunteering for a charity. The question was a strong signal to me that something important was 'off' in this role. On reflection, there was a purpose misalignment, one that proved to be irreconcilable. The problem wasn't that the charity was doing the wrong things. They were doing some brilliant work in poverty relief and social justice. The problem was that my own particular sense of purpose did not connect with the role I had taken on. It was not so much about being outside my comfort zone as a misalignment between what energises and matters to me and what the charity needed from me.

This is the most subjective chapter in this book. It is also arguably the most important. Our leadership proposition is that everyone possesses purpose, at least in potential. Orientating our life's resources towards purposeful activity is crucial for a truly flourishing life. Therefore, for leaders to enable others to flourish, purpose must be high in their thinking. And this thinking is not solely about what's purposeful for the leader. Great leaders enable their people to connect their unique sense of purpose with the needs of the organisation.

What is Purpose?

Purpose can be considered as the point of it all. Not the end destination, but the fundamental reason for anything that we're doing. It's the idea that we matter. That we can make a difference. That we can do some good. That, by applying ourselves to this good, we ourselves will experience the best of what it means to be human.

The idea encompasses meaning and personal values and is unique to every individual, albeit there may be close common themes between us. Purpose is a sense, a feeling, a matter of the heart bubbling within us before it becomes a matter of the mind. Purpose is a whole-of-life thing. Purpose is not necessarily about our work. It's entirely possible to live a highly purposeful life and not do a day's work. Work, if we so choose, is an expression of our sense of purpose, an outlet rather than intrinsically purposeful.

For leaders of people, whilst some vocations may more easily facilitate purposeful activity than others, purpose and meaning can readily be expressed in for-profit, highly commercial environments. In fact, sometimes these provide a wealth of opportunity for meaningful work that does a lot of good. It is also true to say that for some industries this is a stretch to say the least. For example, I find it difficult to locate healthy purpose with the tobacco industry now that the widespread and devastating health impact from smoking is proven.

Our Why

Simon Sinek has done more than most in recent years to elevate the importance of purpose. His book "Start With Why" is a must read. Being clear on why our organisations exist, the purpose and cause that we are pursuing, is crucial to inspiring others, making an impact and creating a living legacy. Purpose, our "why", transcends specific outcomes like making a profit, becoming a CEO, getting one million subscribers. These, whilst (perhaps) important, are secondary. They are outcomes from living and leading with purpose.

Good leaders are able to answer the question, "what's the point?". Great leaders enable their people to understand their individual 'why', too.

Artisans

Purpose evokes the idea that we are all artisans, developing and using our resources and skills to craft and create good outcomes. Outcomes that contribute towards beauty, health, joy, peace and love. Bringing order and form out of chaos and disorder. Enhancing the environment. Making the world, even if only a small part of it, better.

This is not to say that profitability, influence, career progress and other similar measures of success are not important. It is to say that these measures are considered more like symptoms - desirable by-products - of placing purpose and meaning first.

Where purpose comes from is deeply subjective. Some attribute a sense of purpose to the universe, others to God, still others to an innate human trait. But purpose cannot be neatly boxed, defined or measured. Notwithstanding the wealth of research into the importance of a purpose-mindset, whether our proposition is accepted is a matter of belief rather than objective logic. That's perhaps why few business schools elevate purpose in their curriculum and why the idea rarely takes centre stage in leadership meetings, strategic analysis or even operational matters like recruitment and performance management.

Yet without a cause, a core belief, it is difficult - extremely difficult - to lead with excellence, inspire others to meaningful action and create a truly living legacy.

Discovery

What can we do to help clarify our sense of purpose? The first thing to recognise is that purpose is rarely a fixed "thing". It's more a broad sense of our place in the world and how we might make a difference. We can, however, gain some clues.

Understanding our unique style, motivators and strengths can provide some hints. Our particular, characteristics that make us, "us". For example, the more extroverted are likely to find some sense of meaning in more outward activities - directing, socialising, speaking. Crucially, we are wonderfully complex and unique, it takes more than a few minutes of self-reflection or a quick on-line survey to recognise who we truly are.

The activities that we lose ourselves in, where we attain what psychologist Mihaly Csikszentmihalyi termed a state of flow, can help us to discover what's purposeful to us; activity that we find delightful, even when it's demanding. The adage "time flies when you're having fun" points to wisdom. When we're engaged, seeking to accomplish things that are deeply worthwhile, time zips by.

The issues that animate us the most, that we describe ourselves as passionate about can point to purpose. When we reflect back on the situations that have excited, riled and energised us the most, there is often a common thread.

We might notice some ideas from our earlier years, our child-like dreams unencumbered by the constraints of adult realities. These might now seem like naive fantasies and yet we often hear our clients describe some highly meaningful hopes and ambitions from their early years.

Memorable moments can also indicate what, for us, is meaningful. Particular times in our experiences that are etched in our minds and emotions. These may be bad experiences. Sometimes we are propelled to act so that others don't suffer what we have gone through.

However we choose to think about purpose, it cannot be relegated to our scarce spare time or ignored entirely. Whether on our own or with trusted friends or a coach, giving ourselves quality time to consider, refine and dwell on what makes life and our activity meaningful will underpin the quality of our life and leadership.

Noticing

Ales Bialiatski was awarded the Nobel Peace Prize in 2022 for his life and work in promoting democracy and human rights in Belarus, a country that frequently jails people who protest against its authoritarian government, including Ales himself. Ales joins a long list of inspiring people and organisations who have received the prize since its inception in 1901.

The Nobel prizes were established by the will of Alfred Nobel, a Swedish industrialist. What's remarkable is that Nobel's primary industry and source of wealth was far more closely associated with war than peace. Alfred Nobel is credited with inventing dynamite, developing explosives and armaments. What might have motivated Nobel to gift his fortune for the furtherment of humanity?

It's speculation, but there's a very good chance that a monumental press faux pas was a catalyst. Alfred's brother died in France from a heart attack and, apparently, one French newspaper misreported that it was Alfred who had died. They printed a devastating obituary, branding him a merchant of death, profiting from finding ways to mutilate and kill. According to biographer Kenne Fant, Nobel "became so obsessed with the posthumous reputation that he rewrote his last will, bequeathing most of his fortune to a cause upon which no future obituary writer would be able to cast aspersions."

Excellent leaders notice. They notice the impact they are making on others and in the world. They orientate their effort to making a positive difference, one that carries meaning and purpose. Alfred Nobel gives us a dramatic example of a leader being forced to notice. The feedback provided via the misplaced - yet honest - obituary influenced his legacy in ways that we continue to benefit from. Purpose-fuelled leaders are keenly self-aware. They reflect on their true motives for their decisions and actions. Recognising how easy it is for anyone to become blind to their own faults, they seek external, honest feedback. They are determined to stay on the right path.

Five Whys

"I've realised that I've been climbing the wrong mountain". That was the statement made by a CEO who had made it to the top of their global corporate. In a moment of clarity, they recognised that their pursuit of career advancement had served very little joy and robbed them of family, friends and contentment. Having attained status, they realised that they had achieved very little of true meaning. Have you felt similar in your working career? Perhaps this resonates with you even as you're reading these sentences.

It's remarkable to us the number of people we meet who have spent a significant proportion of their time working hard in careers and roles who lack any strong sense of purpose. The reasons seem to vary. Some are too busy to think about why they're so busy. Others have inflated their definition of the amount needed for financial security and stayed in boring yet high paying jobs. Still others have postponed their plans to do the things they really want to do until an arbitrary date in the future, "I'll retire from this job in five years and then pursue more interesting things". We observe one common theme amongst them. They seem disappointed, regretful, a little lost.

They - we all - know deep down when we are giving ourselves to things that are not purposeful for us.

The key to a flourishing life and excellent leadership is focus. Focussing our energy and resources on activity that contributes to something meaningful. Focussing the resources of the organisations that we lead into actions that contribute to something meaningful. Ensuring that our people understand the fundamental point of what we're asking them to do. Inspiring them with a bigger idea, one that makes tackling today's issues worthwhile.

Here's where the five whys can help us. Persistently asking "why?" up to five times ahead of any commitment, or in response to ideas presented to us, helps us to drill down to the core purpose. It might go something like this:

- I'm reading this book. Why?

- To learn something and be a better leader. Why?

- So that I can lead my people and organisation even better. Why?

- So that we can achieve great results and enjoy our work together. Why?

- If we achieve our aims, many more people will have easy access to healthcare (replace with your company's big-picture aim). Aha! Now we have something purposeful.

Applying five whys to your strategic imperatives, tactics, meetings (too many meetings are devoid of anything purposeful) and daily tasks will ensure that you and the organisation you lead is working towards truly important impact and outcomes. You might even consider a to-don't list. If, after asking 'why?' five times you're not convinced that there's a good fundamental reason for the action or issue in scope, that becomes something not-to-do. Our time and resources are limited; deciding what not to do, or what not to do anymore, is just as important as deciding what must be done. Pursuing new or persisting with current activity that doesn't connect with purpose is a symptom of poor leadership.

Our last thought on this point is this. It is possible and indeed likely that our sense of purpose in life is broader than just one field. We locate meaning in faith, friendships, family and work that serves others. When asking the five whys, our answers will illuminate a deeper and broader spectrum of what makes life meaningful.

Soul

At the root of the word 'passion' is the idea of suffering. That there is a compelling cause worthy of our heart, mind and soul. Without purpose, hard work becomes soul destroying. We occasionally hear people lament that they've given their life and soul to the organisations they've worked for. With purpose, our dedication and passion fuels our personal growth and propels us to bring life and soul to the people in our lives.

Don't sell your soul, feed it.

Horizon thinking is thinking to the finish. It's seeking to understand today's choices from the perspective of a bigger picture, perhaps one that extends even beyond our tenure.

Chapter 12
Legacy-Minded Leaders
Think Beyond the Horizon

Legacy minded leaders are dedicated to the future.

I love a task list. I write mine in physical form, sometimes beautifully arranged in my notebook, at other times hastily sketched out on post it notes. Lists help prompt my actions, prioritise my tasks and give me a sense of accomplishment. Everyone should use lists.

Yet, there's a serious problem for leaders when it comes to lists. Yes, getting through the tasks is important; meeting a shareholder, recruiting a COO, negotiating with a supplier, agreeing a brand strategy. But if those tasks are not connected intimately with something bigger - working towards a better future, one that carries meaning - then all the activity loses its impact. There is no gravitas to the work, no real buy-in, lots of busyness but not much lasting satisfaction. It's a recipe for either burnout or apathy, neither of which is desirable or healthy.

What's needed is horizon thinking. The desire and ability to imagine a profoundly better future. One that the leader's organisation can contribute towards with the right effort and dedication. Something that's meaningful, that makes the world a better place. Something enduring, important and beyond just-a-job. It is defined more in terms of future impact than mechanics. "An end to homelessness in our neighbourhood", "equality of access to education", "freedom of artistic expression" are all examples.

Then (and only then) designing pathways - products, services, actions - towards that future. At the same time, holding those plans lightly enough to flex as unpredicted situations arise, always with the long-term, meaningful goal in mind. Rallying the organisation towards this bigger idea whilst enabling focussed effort towards achieving it - that's true leadership.

Task lists born of such a vision are powerful!

Overcoming Short-Termism

Modern business thinking has placed efficiency - fully optimising resources and eliminating anything wasteful - as central to strategic action. Optimising resources is a good thing; achieving excellence in any setting requires efficiency. However, when the pursuit of efficiency becomes an objective in itself, a reason for existence and more than a strategic tool, the conditions are set for decisions that are destructive for your legacy.

Consider the CEO of a public company who is obsessed by hitting continual growth in the company's quarterly revenue numbers. They set constant growth expectations with shareholders and then adopt an acute sensitivity to the share price, which becomes, to them, a barometer of their personal success and value. Despite the logic and reason that consistent quarterly growth is extremely unlikely over the long run, the CEO becomes determined to deliver growth every single time.

In an effort to preserve their personal reputation and perceived value, the CEO starts to massage the numbers, first in small ways. "We'll hold back some of that revenue for a future quarter" in a good period. "We'll start to bill customers up front and book all the revenue now" in a weak quarter. Massage escalates to manipulation. "We can extend the write off period for our fixed assets". "We can shift those liabilities off-balance sheet". "Let's slash our intra company loan interest rates". "We don't need to book in those costs yet, we might get away with it later in the year". Everything in the company is objectified, a number that contributes towards or detracts from the quarterly targets. Customers, employees, suppliers - everyone - is simply a means to a numerical end. Short termist leaders defend their decisions aggressively and then bask in the perceived applause from shareholders, regardless of any collateral damage caused along the way.

Here we arrive at what seems like a contradiction. Achieving great results - financial performance, quadrupling the share price, constructing the tallest buildings, winning an Oscar, firing a rocket to the moon - sounds like a great legacy. Certainly these types of accolades would pave the way for conference speaking, press interviews and book writing. And yet, whilst achievements such as these can be worthwhile, they pale in comparison with the legacy that we leave with the people that we have impacted. Our colleagues, friends, family, employees, customers, communities. Every encounter with another person is an opportunity to build a living legacy. Every decision that impacts on people - even those whom we will never meet - is an opportunity to build a truly living legacy.

It is impossible to objectify people and build a living legacy at the same time. If you are to be obsessed by anything, be obsessed by the lives of the people you are impacting, not by short-term quarterly results.

The Corps of Discovery

In 1804, Meriwether Lewis and William Clark and their 'Corps of Discovery' of forty people set off to find the elusive and as it turns out, mythical, river passage across America to the Pacific Ocean. Their story is one of team leadership at its utmost, packed with exemplary insight into enduring leadership qualities.

Picture the scene. Lewis, Clark and their team had arrived at the source of the Missouri river after many months of arduous expedition. Received wisdom was that this would mark the peak mountain range, with a river flowing West to the Pacific Ocean. Discovery of this route would, it was believed, catalyse a new golden era of trade. As Lewis and Clark reached the source of the Missouri, canoes in hand, they were faced not with a sloping plain and rivers down towards the Pacific but with the ominous Rocky Mountains. Unexpected. Unsuitable for canoes. Unmapped.

What would you do? The Corps of Discovery adapted, repurposed their canoes and pressed on over the mountains. Undoubtedly, they were horizon thinkers. They were possessed by a grand idea, a vision and passion for a better future. This transcended detailed plans and precise maps (there were none). Daily tasks flexed and changed but always in the pursuit of the grand idea. Even when faced with the shocking truth that their presumptions were wrong, The Corps of Discovery continued on with their "big picture" mission of finding a trade route to the Pacific.

All organisations can - and must - have some sense of meaningful future objective, to motivate through hurdles and pressures that will arise. It is fundamentally the role of the leader to constantly nurture and convey the meaning, the grand idea, of everything their organisation exists for.

Think to the Finish

"Think to the finish" is a famous adage of Field Marshal Allenby. He sought to convey the idea that officers should think beyond the boundaries of their immediate command and consider the wider consequence and the context in which they were in. Otherwise, they might win their particular fight but risk losing the battle (or worse).

We can learn a lot from this idea. In our leadership, it can be seemingly easy to focus our attention on our own success, with scant regard for the impact on our colleagues and wider organisation, let alone the communities and even world in which we're placed. We may congratulate ourselves on winning but fail to see the wider costs that we've inflicted.

Horizon thinking is thinking to the finish. It's seeking to understand today's choices from the perspective of a bigger picture, perhaps one that extends even beyond our tenure. It's asking, "how will this decision contribute to the grander plan?" and acting with the larger objective, not necessarily the immediate win, in mind.

End of History Illusion

This future minded approach may sound obvious, but as is the case for all leadership wisdom, it is not quite so easy in practice. The best ideas are nearly always simple but never easy. It takes intention and courage to stay focussed on the horizon.

Psychologists have identified that we humans underestimate the future. We are biased towards what we know and have experienced, rather than what we don't yet know. This includes our perspective on our own values and preferences. When asked to think forward, we don't believe that we will change much, yet when asked to reflect backwards, we recognise that we have in fact changed a lot.

This is called an 'end of history illusion' and as social psychologist Dan Gilbert puts it, "...we overpay for the opportunity to indulge our current preferences because we overestimate their stability..." We prefer the ease of remembering over the difficulty of imagining. Even without the science, we know this anecdotally to be true. I know what I like now and therefore project that into the future, despite knowing that some of my preferences have changed - quite substantially - over my lifetime.

Extending this idea to leading our people, it is easier to assume that past and present experiences will continue without significant change, than to imagine disruption or a substantially different operating environment. On top of that, future thinking tends to incur criticism rather than encouragement. People's tendency to prefer stability and seek the familiar creates a natural resistance to horizon ideas; the lack of certainty is, by definition, risky. Addressing criticism whilst still pressing forward takes courage - it's a harder path than pleasing our critics.

It can sometimes take a shock to the system to force us to change. The covid pandemic delivered just such a shock, accelerating underlying trends including working from home, home food deliveries, subscriptions to digital entertainment to name just a few. The rapid adoption of these changes was barely considered and mostly dismissed before the pandemic. In the months before the pandemic, one of our CEO clients remarked that "at best, a maximum of one-third of our people can work flexibly from home." Within three weeks of the first lockdown, the company was operating fully with all employees working from home. They achieved record results during those months.

This serves to illustrate how pervasive the end of history illusion is. It constrains our imagination and therefore our planning. It takes effort to think-forward, it's not easy to do. Leaders must give themselves - their time and energy - to thinking to the horizon.

Beliefs

How can we identify if we're too short-sighted? Fixed statements of opinion presented as fact are strong signals and should alarm us. Statements of belief that include the words "always", or "never"; "can't be done" or "that's just what we do" indicate that we have lost sight of the horizon. Especially when noticed in the same sentence.

"We will never achieve that...."

"Our customers will never buy that...."

"We will always have this product...."

"We can't do that. We will never have the time to...."

"We can't change that, our shareholders always demand....."

It's not that these types of statement are necessarily untrue. It's that, if they're left untested, they become true by default and constrain our ability to think to the horizon. Worse, when our limiting beliefs become entrenched, we put our precious resources to work towards a future that looks practically the same as the present. That's called management - maintaining the status quo - not leadership.

Do you have any "never", "always", "can't" beliefs about the future of your organisation? Are you willing to let them go? How will you test these to understand which are no longer true and limiting your horizons?

Hallmarks of a Horizon Thinker

There are the three hallmarks of the horizon thinker. Can you recognise these in yourself?

- Horizon thinkers are adventurous. They are excited to discover new ideas. They are curious and energised by the unexpected. "Same old" is demotivating and dull to them. What's gone before might inform a decision, but familiar methods are not presumed to be the best approach. They embrace the idea that the future cannot be predicted with a high degree of certainty and enjoy the idea that uncertainty is the very condition that adds immense value to life and work. The energy associated with adventure is infectious and motivating to others.

- Horizon thinkers respond calmly to both successes and problems. They don't react with drama. This is because leaders with a big idea have a constant "press forward" mindset. They celebrate successes for a moment and then move on. They commiserate failures for a moment and then move on. They recognise milestones - both good and bad - but don't live there; they are focussed on the horizon. Incidents along the journey are therefore held in their proper context and don't become all-consuming.

- Horizon thinkers hold relational capital in very high regard. They understand that meaningful outcomes cannot be achieved through one person's skills and efforts alone. They don't simply invite external perspectives, they weave together - via genuine relationships - diverse skills and experiences into their teams.

Taking the Corps of Discovery as our case study example, Lewis and Clark led the Corps as co-captains, despite different ranks being awarded to them. This set the tone for the whole Corps. They fostered and valued trusting relationships, respecting differences including with people who, at the time, would have been considered "lesser" and certainly surprising colleagues and influencers (their story is well worth a read).

"He who travels alone travels fastest, but in the company of friends you go farther."

Fostering a living legacy requires a future focus. This is not to ignore the past completely; our history can be informative. But, if we are to lead well, the past and even the present cannot dominate our thoughts. It's the future that's in scope for excellent leaders. The best leaders lift the eyes of their people upwards and inspire them forwards.

THE LEADERS BOOK

Leadership is not a solo sport. Leaders do not arrive in a leadership role without input from others.

Chapter 13
Legacy-Minded Leaders
Make Leaders not just Followers

In a world where success is often measured by monetary value or popularity and how many likes or how many followers you have on Twitter or LinkedIn...Leaders need to keep their focus on what really matters. We started off this section on legacy by exploring purpose and how all our actions and decisions need to come from our why, otherwise they are likely just a distraction and will dilute the impact of our real work and purpose.

However, there is a purpose that is shared by all leaders, but not all leaders choose to take up the challenge of fulfilling this universal purpose. This will be a familiar phrase to you I am sure, but that doesn't make it less important or more dismissible - Tom Peters says, "Great leaders don't create followers, they create more leaders". Because great leaders see beyond the end of their tenure, they are driven by a purpose greater than their own needs and wants that must surely require them to pass the baton on to someone else who can finish the race they started or at least move closer to the goal before handing the baton to someone else. And great leaders have a people first mindset, they understand that by caring for their people they are caring for their organisation.

We would say that leaders who are content to settle for followers only, demonstrate laziness and self-centredness. Why? These leaders think only of the short-term wins, not the longer-term purpose and vision of the organisation.

Let's face it, being a good leader is tough, it takes time, effort, intention, practice, commitment and more. We sometimes hear leaders say they don't have time to invest in growing other leaders, that's the HR department's job - these leaders are wrong. Looking to the future success of the organisation - be it business, charity, or even a religious establishment, leaders need to look beyond their tenure, beyond the bottom line, or the share price on the day they walk out the door for the final time.

But how can you create more leaders?

Be the Best Leader you Can Be

We only need to read headlines in the news or on social media to know that leaders are watched and noticed whether they realise it or not. Potential leaders will be especially attentive to how leaders lead, so quite simply - lead yourself well! Be self-aware, conscious of the behaviours and attitudes you are modelling. Remember as a leader, your words, your actions, your reactions all matter, they will set the culture and inform any future leader in your organisation what you think good leadership looks like.

Be inspiring! Demonstrate the positive impact that leadership can have, and the qualities needed to be a great leader.

Let people know that there is life outside of the office or workplace. This isn't about oversharing, it is about modelling good boundaries, not sending emails late into the night, taking proper annual leave, taking time to prioritise family. More than ever people are looking for leadership that respects and appreciates their lives are multi-faceted - that's inspiring too.

Being a great leader in itself will not only inspire those within your organisation, it will also attract brilliant people to join your organisation.

Become a Talent Scout!

In the earlier chapter "Embrace your defining moments", we read about a haematologist in training who changed the course of their career to become a virologist and eventually lead a community through the Covid-19 pandemic because she was so impacted by the words of a leader in her field who she highly respected. I imagine that leader identified some potential within the insightful student standing before him.

As leaders we have the privilege and responsibility to take notice and to look for potential and emerging leaders. This will demand some of your time, energy and creativity but may also be a brilliant opportunity to involve others in too. Identify projects or responsibilities that will stretch and challenge those you are seeking to develop - encourage them and give them space to find solutions in their own way, to think for themselves, not just how they have seen you solve problems.

Cultivate habits that make you aware of your people, their skills and aptitudes. If your organisation is too big for you to do this personally, make sure your vision and strategy for creating more leaders is clearly known and followed by other leaders in your organisation so they can be your eyes and ears.

The Importance of Coaching and Mentoring

Leadership is not a solo sport. Leaders do not arrive in a leadership role without input from others. Think about your life and your career, who has been most influential in your development? Most likely there have been many people in different seasons and at different stages of your life who have encouraged you, guided you, challenged you and inspired you. Perhaps you can trace these positive influences back to childhood and recognise the impact parents or grandparents had, perhaps teachers and youth leaders, and as you continue on through life - colleagues, managers, community leaders and friends. Maybe you have even invested in being coached or have had a trusted mentor who has spoken into your life, shared their knowledge, wisdom and experience with you and encouraged and challenged you. I bet there are many people who have come into your mind, many people who have walked with you through different periods of your life. Those influences, those relationships have all contributed to your success - how are you contributing to the success of a leader or leaders who will come after you?

If you choose to mentor emerging leaders, or coach as part of your role, you will need to demonstrate a degree of vulnerability. Part of being an inspirational leader is being able to acknowledge your own weaknesses, own your mistakes, share your learning, and being authentic is essential. Having the confidence and humility to bring your whole self to work and be really seen is powerful. Emerging leaders need to know what's required of a leader - not just status, salary and a title. Will you allow them to see and understand integrity or moral courage in action? If we were talking about engines, they would need to understand how the engine works, what its limitations were and so on - not just that you turn the ignition and we're off!

Power

We briefly explored power in the earlier chapter "Share Power' as we were thinking about empowerment. We need to think about power from the perspective of growing other leaders too. There's a wonderful quote from Martin Luther King in 1967, "... Power properly understood is nothing but the ability to achieve purpose. It is the strength required to bring about social, political, and economic change." Leaders need power to achieve their purpose, which is hopefully for a greater good, a greater purpose than themselves. As leaders, we need to demonstrate the proper use of power, the morally courageous use of power, power wielded with integrity. It is a leader's responsibility to do this.

Beware of fast-track schemes though, especially if they are perceived as, or actually are, short cuts. We do future leaders a disservice if we remove challenges and barriers that really remove development opportunities (this is not the same as removing barriers to equality) The author and researcher, Margaret Heffernan has written on the three problems of power. In the first one she recounts the story of an incredibly intelligent engineer who rises quickly through promotions. Problems arise when he reaches the top levels in the business and he comes across a problem that he doesn't know how to solve - there was a culture problem with a colleague breaching ethical guidelines and others knowing about it, but not challenging it. This brilliant young man had never been taught how to use the power that he had. He had never had to seek out or fight for promotions, they had always been offered. Crucially he had never been taught to think for himself, or challenge leaders.

It isn't unusual for people who are brilliant in their field to be promoted into management and leadership positions - they have superb knowledge and skills, their experience is invaluable, they have earned the promotion through hard work, dedication and long hours. And yet, they have no experience in leading people or organisations, no experience of how to apply their values in this way, little self-awareness and are then left floundering.

Leaders who make leaders use their power to identify and nurture talent within the organisation. They ensure that there is investment in an individual's growth as a leader, and not only an excellent employee.

Be a Prospector

The whole process of leaders making leaders reminds me of this great adage "Be the one to find the gold in people." The implication is that it's easier to find the dirt, or the fault. But indulge me as I stretch the imagery further. As leaders our task doesn't end at finding the gold, we may need to take on the role of helping to refine the gold. Refining traditionally was done by melting the gold over high heat, during the process impurities would come to the surface and could be skimmed off, leaving a purer, better-quality gold below. As leaders how can we turn up the heat and help to create opportunities, "sweaty" moments, for aspiring leaders to test themselves, take risks, make mistakes and then help them learn from those moments in order to hone not just their skills but their character?

This will take some thought and some risk. . .but here are a few pitfalls to avoid, a few ways to surely fail at this goal of creating more leaders:

- Focus on targets not people. When leaders fail to focus on the people in their organisation and instead shift all their attention on the targets, the bottom line, the kudos, it would be like builders focusing on contracting the building and missing out the foundations, it won't last!

- Being a perfectionist (i.e. not a risk taker, not accepting of mistakes) Perfectionism suffocates creativity, turns leaders into micromanagers and control freaks! And as Brenè Brown puts it "When perfectionism is driving us, shame is riding shotgun and fear is that annoying backseat driver!"

- Making it all about you - ego and pride will almost certainly constrain you, and it will certainly repel brilliant, talented and morally courageous emerging leaders.

- Not cultivating a growth mindset - not acknowledging or promoting your own need for growth and development.

Creating a living legacy includes developing excellent future leaders. People who will overtake you, who make more of a difference than you, who leave to lead their own organisations, who themselves become sought-after mentors for the next generation.

THE LEADERS BOOK

A living legacy mindset always considers the impact of our choices, decisions, and actions.

Chapter 14
Legacy-Minded Leaders
Consider Whole-Community Impact

Everything we do matters. Because everything we do has an impact. The impact may be very small and seemingly insignificant, but nonetheless there's an impact. As leaders, we must be ever mindful that our actions and behaviours can have an effect on other people, and that's not always just limited to some others, but potentially at times *all* others. We may never know or see the full results or repercussions of what we do, but that doesn't mean they're not there.

Any living legacy minded leader will have this in their thoughts, as a forethought, not an afterthought. Everything in the world is intimately interconnected. The opinion that we are in our small corner, doing our small thing and therefore it matters not in the greater scheme of things, is a woefully misguided opinion.

It is essentially the butterfly effect.

Linked to the Chaos theory and attributed to mathematician and meteorologist Edward Lorenz, this is the idea that small things can have an impact on a complex system. Like the wings of a butterfly flapping and causing a typhoon. Though this one small event would not actually cause the typhoon, the single event can be the catalyst that acts on starting conditions.

James Baldwin epitomises this wonderfully in "The Horseshoe nails", based on a proverb from the 13th century:

"For the want of a nail the shoe was lost;

For the want of a shoe the horse was lost;

For the want of a horse the battle was lost;

For the failure of battle the kingdom was lost; -

And all for the want of a horseshoe nail."

The loss of a horseshoe nail could be of no significance, or it could indirectly cause the loss of a war and kingdom.

As Terry Pratchett and Neil Gaiman write in their book Good Omens, "It used to be thought that the events that changed the world were things like big bombs, maniac politicians, huge earthquakes, or vast population movements, but it has now been realised that this is a very old-fashioned view held by people totally out of touch with modern thought. The things that change the world, according to Chaos theory, are the tiny things."

A living legacy mindset always considers the impact of our choices, decisions, and actions. Considering only ourselves, our time, our moment, our success, and our comfort is for yesterday's thinking. We as leaders have a responsibility to lead holistically in our approach.

What impact are your choices and actions having on those that you love, the stakeholders in your organisation, the local community you live in, and the global community to which you are a part of? At the heart of any living legacy has to be the influence we have on the communities we are a part of. While we are the leader of an organisation, we can have an impact on all of them, as well as leaving an impact that will outlast us.

During the global pandemic of 2020 people observed that there was a real sense of community spirit. There was a feeling of involvement and shared concern for not just the immediate community that people lived in, but the wider global community as well. This may be the one thing that people look back on with favourable memories, the sense of community, being connected with others.

And it is community that businesses are now realising more than ever grows healthy and successful organisations. Of course, this is no new idea. Religion throughout the ages has emphasised the need of humanity for connection, relationships, giving and serving others, the need to belong and be part of something and we'd be wise to heed such wisdom. We can so often get caught up in many other things and neglect the most basic of human needs - community.

The world we live in is wired up for community and the best way for us to flourish as a society is to be interconnected, all recognising and acknowledging that we all have a part to play, especially when we are in a position of influence. And, connections will help us to grow and change, they will challenge our thinking and get us to reassess ways in which we have always done things, as well as affording us nurture and encouragement.

The Community Within

The community we build within our organisation is essential. People need to feel part of something bigger than themselves, and not just feel like they're working in isolation. All people and all departments are together, not in competition but working and contributing for the company as a whole. People don't want to just play their part but see how their part fits together with all the others.

Building community within starts with trustworthy leadership which subsequently means building trustworthy teams and creating psychologically safe environments. This of course, as outlined throughout the book, includes giving everyone a voice, strengthening relationships and having excellent communication. But how else are we to foster great connections within?

Team bonds can be strengthened by creating workspaces for people to talk, share ideas and work collaboratively. Team building and social events could be part of the culture, but more thought and creativity are needed, to avoid the mundane. From day one people need to begin to feel part of something. And this can be said of any organisation, establishment, or group. The first day for a student at school, the first time a person walks into a social club, church family, or moves into a neighbourhood. How are we personally impacting a person's first impressions?

Onboarding in the workplace should be a priority and should be done to the highest of standards. A person should go home after the first day enthused and energised by the purpose, values and people of the company. Don't just delegate this task with little thought, give onboarding top attention. The first day matters greatly.

The Customer and Consumer Community

It is not just about building a product anymore, or selling an idea, whether that be a mobile device, an educational system, a cause or religious belief, but rather it is about building a community where people come together around it. There is consumer buy in, and members of this community enthuse one another, support each other and recruit new members.

Technology has opened up a whole new door for us on this, as no longer do people have to go to a physical place to meet up to share their love of a particular product or company. But emails and newsletters alone won't cut it, people are looking for something more meaningful, a deeper more purposeful connection. A member community can provide this.

Caring about the customer and the consumer means we have to care about the local and global community that we serve, for today people are making significant choices based on how connected and ethical companies are. How are we doing with this?

The Local Community

All organisations have an integral role to play in the wider community and society, and because businesses have many relationships and responsibilities with and towards a range of stakeholders the impact and influence can be vast.

Connecting with the local community can be both a form of charity and an organisational strategy. I would argue that it is our duty to do what we can to help, support and give where possible to good causes and to get involved in local community matters in order to help the community thrive and flourish. There is an expectation especially on businesses to give something back, but there is also real benefit for any business, company, or organisation with regards to marketing, promotion, profit, employee engagement and more.

Connecting to a local community project or venture will boost business by exposure and affiliation to a good or charitable cause. It helps to demonstrate what your organisation stands for and what's important, it can reveal your trustworthiness, reliability, and generosity. It could be argued that this is also a way to beat your competition, but at *Leaders* we would encourage a different mindset, not one that is out to beat the competition but rather out last it, and community connections contribute to longevity.

It can be tempting for the leaders of charitable and religious organisations to feel that because they are doing good for the community in and of themselves that there is no need for them to support other good causes or get involved in other local community matters, but we would argue that this is an impoverished mindset. In fact, the competitive spirit is often just as prevalent in charities and churches as is presumed with for-profit businesses. Charity leaders can become excessively focussed on winning funding and church leaders on growing their congregations even if this is at the expense of other charities and churches. Leaders with a living legacy mindset instead consider the whole community impact, sometimes making decisions that benefit other organisations over their own if that's in the best interests of the community that they're serving. They are secure people and see other organisations as potential partners rather than competitors. They support other groups rather than copy (or undermine) their initiatives. Charities helping and supporting other great causes and issues, religious communities giving outside of themselves, has far reaching benefits for all concerned. Legacy is about ensuring long-lasting impact, so the more people work together, the more unity is displayed, the more good can be attained and the more positive change can be achieved.

What sort of impact are we making in our local community?

The Global Community

It is important to recognise ourselves as far more than just a part of a local community however, we are part of a global community too and our neighbour extends to a far greater reach than the person literally across the road. The 'our community first' mentality has always seemed a bizarre one. If we live in a world where we do in fact believe that all people are born equal and free, then suffice to say, whether we are engaged locally or globally is of equal value.

There has definitely been a shift over the last decade with a rise in social justice awareness. From issues concerning human rights and animal rights through to environmental concerns, the human race is awakening more and more, little by little, to the world-wide issues that are before us in both the present and the future.

When we look back in history on the things that used to be done and accepted, I wonder today about what in years to come we will look back on, shocked at ourselves for being so blinded, for holding certain beliefs, or allowing particular practices to continue. Though we are slowly realising the mistakes made with regards to equality, fair-trade and the environment we still have a long way to go. Our organisations have the opportunity to make great positive contributions to such matters, which ultimately means *we* have the opportunity to make great positive contributions.

How connected are our companies with global issues? Do we care about issues of sustainability, our carbon footprint, the rights and treatment of not just all stakeholders but humanity as a whole? What is the legacy we are creating and leaving? We cannot just leave it to other people and other places. We have to realise that what we do, has a much wider impact then we might initially recognise. We cannot be ignorant anymore. Gone are the days when a leader can claim that they were unaware of ill treatment of employees in impoverished work conditions and therefore not own any responsibility.

Everybody on Board

Get the whole organisation involved and make community involvement both locally and globally part of the fabric of the company. Token gestures whilst having some value, don't really cut it. Because if integrity really matters to us, this has to go beyond just making us or the organisation look good. For a business to be truly ethical, social responsibility needs to be integrated into all of its practices.

Part of helping with the building of community within as mentioned previously, is by getting people to look to the community outside. Bringing people together with a shared common vision and purpose for a greater good, strengthens relationships between people but also it creates a fabulous opportunity for joy; looking beyond ourselves and our day-to-day work. This meaningful engagement inspires and empowers and will boost people's morale, subsequently producing greater productivity. In addition to this, community engagement attracts great employees because many people today will favour working for or being part of something that has values that align with their own.

It's Really Up to Us!

When people say that business has a social responsibility, this really implies that leaders of businesses have a responsibility. That is us. We are the ones to drive our organisations forward, and lead in such a way that enhances wider society. It is not just all about us, in our little corner. We are one piece of a global puzzle, and it is imperative that we do our part in making the picture complete and beautiful.

We will have an impact on all of these communities. The real question is what type of impact do we want that to be?

A living legacy has no place for solo journeying.

It is one of connection.

One of community.

One that cares.

THE LEADERS BOOK

Joy is not found in the promotion of a false happiness, or fake positivity. Joy is genuine and should be intrinsic within a company. It should flow through the bloodstream of an organisation.

Chapter 15
Legacy-Minded Leaders
Spread the Joy!

A Culture of Joy

How many of us as leaders are in pursuit of joy? We often find ourselves in pursuit of performance, results, profit, promotion, but joy ... I'm not sure whether that would be the first thing that springs to mind, if at all. But perhaps we're missing a trick here. What if it is in the pursuit of joy that we get spurred on further in our attainment of all of the above. What if joy propels us forward and acts as a catalyst?

Just in the same way that Burt Bacharach and Hal David declared that the world needed more love, I wonder today whether what the workplace needs now is joy, more joy! I'm convinced that in many places there really is just too little of it. Many people get the very real sense of the 'Sunday night dread feeling.' If we want this to change, which I assume we all would, then what is to be done? How can we ensure as leaders, that our people want to come to work or to the establishment we are running, and more than that, they look forward to it?

Perhaps joy is one component of that answer. As we consider our living legacy, part of this must include joy, because joy is the result of getting other things right. Joy is not some airy fairy, wishy washy, fluffy notion that finds its place outside of the 'serious' work world, it should be right smack bang in the middle of the workplace, and should be the outflow from our culture, strategy and vision. Joy should be embraced and harnessed, for it has transformational power.

Who we are and what we do as a leader will be instrumental in contributing towards the culture of our organisation. We will shape culture through conscious and unconscious actions, behaviours and decisions. Everything within this book is about being and doing things that will define culture, from who we are to what we do. But how do we know that we're setting the cultural tone right, how do we measure this? Well perhaps it would be worth looking at how joyful our people are, from employees to customers and everyone in between.

When we have the right ingredients, we will see the evidence of this in greater satisfaction, and better general well-being. Great culture after all is not about giving lots of bonuses and rewards and 'free stuff' but actually great culture is all about how people feel. Nothing can compensate for how people feel.

There is much debate about the difference between joy and happiness which has led to the forming of various opinions, but joy for me is perhaps something bigger than happiness. Happiness can come and go and is dependent on the moment, whereas joy transcends this and stays constant throughout each moment.

Happiness is ephemeral, joy is lasting. Within any working environment, it would be impossible to maintain super high levels of happiness all the time; disappointments, sadness, frustrations, anger will of course arise, whether that be directly related to professional reasons or personal ones. However, joy can still sit alongside these feelings and reside in the same space. Joy at work, a culture of joy, does not equate with just a sense of frivolity and jubilation, though those things I would argue can be a part of it, rather joy goes way beyond to give people a real sense of contentment, purpose, meaning, belonging and satisfaction.

Joy is not just about the emotions we exhibit; it runs deeper than this. Joy is birthed from meaningful connections. That can be a connection with the work that we are involved in or with the people we work with. When these positive connections abound, so joy follows, even in the face of great adversity. It is a leader's job to help create those connections for people. Joy is not found in the promotion of a false happiness, or fake positivity. Joy is genuine and should be intrinsic within a company. It should flow through the bloodstream of an organisation.

At 'Leaders' we ultimately exist to equip those in positions of leadership to create and foster healthy, high performing workplaces, where people thrive and enjoy their work. It is not only about successful productivity but about creating a culture of joy which leads to flourishing in all areas. In this book we have outlined what we believe are the contributing factors to enabling such an ambition. Joy is the best expression of it all.

Joyfully Purposed and Psychologically Safe

The importance of purpose is paramount as we have just recently read about. When people know their purpose in an organisation and know the organisation's purpose, there is far greater job satisfaction; people want to be involved in meaningful work.

To be joyfully purposed also encompasses feeling empowered and valued. A misuse of power or where power is sought for power's sake, only leads to low trust, high blame, frustration and often misery. Reflecting on our work with leaders and leadership teams in a wide variety of settings, where companies genuinely empower and encourage others, take responsibility for failings, are open to feedback and seek to advance the careers of as many people as possible, there is a positive and joyful culture that exists. Emotional well-being is far higher when people know that they are in a place where they can speak out without humiliation, take risks and make mistakes without punishment. The most engaged, productive and joyous workers feel psychologically safe.

An absence of joy in any organisation should be a warning sign that something is not right.

Moving Beyond the Core Principles

Whilst real and lasting joy at work is based on all that we have outlined in this book, there is a part of a joyful culture that extends to more visible factors.

Celebrate

Everyone loves a party! Well, ok not everyone, but that's probably more to do with what type of party is being thrown. People generally like to celebrate. The question we need to ask ourselves is what are we celebrating and who are we celebrating?

Our organisations should be full of celebration. Whether it's celebrating a corporate success or team success, or if it's a particular individual achievement, we should be sharing good news all the time and celebrating it. Positive moments, stories, ideas and achievements will be all around the office, we just have to capture them and raise their profile.

There is always something to be celebrated, even in the mistakes and the disasters, there are often moments, or specific attainments or people, to be celebrated if we just look hard enough. The way a team handles a particular problem or challenge may be worth applause or the honesty with which a person held their hands up, or the way someone used a mistake to propel them forward. Seek and ye shall find!

Fuel the Fun

As leaders we don't have to be 'Captain Fun Times' day in day out, to which we all breathe a sigh of relief. However, we do need to appreciate that the tone of our organisations is set very much by us. If we are negative, moody, grumpy, angry then we can't expect much more from our people.

It's important to think about what we're portraying to others. Do we exhibit joy? Your impact and influence is so much greater than you realise. Obviously, some of us are more naturally inclined to having a joyful demeanour, but even those of us who aren't, we can still choose the way we come across to others. How we act, respond, what we say; there are infinite opportunities for joy.

Aesthetically Aware

Physical environments matter. Even if you're not personally too concerned about soft furnishings the likelihood is that most of us will appreciate good surroundings when we're in them and we may be surprised to discover what impact they might actually have on us. When we consider what universally brings us joy, surely we would have to agree that it is nature that unites. And we only have to look at the natural world with all its colour and vibrancy to realise that this beauty cultivates in us a sense of lightness and joy. So, if this is the case why do our workspaces so often reflect the exact opposite of such beauty?

In this last decade there has been a real shift in perspective when it comes to the work environment. The benefit of investment in physical furnishings is being recognised. Not only can it help with productivity, but it shows people that they are valued and that their comfort and well-being matter too. A joyful environment and culture is holistically minded.

Gratefully Appreciate

It is a well acknowledged truth that joyfulness and gratefulness are connected. Mistakenly we can think that it is joy that makes us grateful but actually it's the other way around, gratitude brings us joy. Gratitude produces more positive emotions, so it stands to reason that if we want to have more joy in our own lives and create a joyful culture, then we need to cultivate a grateful and appreciative attitude. For not only does gratitude make us feel better, it is pretty much guaranteed to make someone else feel better too if they are being thanked and appreciated. It is not enough to be satisfied with just feeling grateful, but we have to actively practice gratefulness, especially towards others.

Joy is everything!

'Leaders' as an organisation exists to inspire and equip leaders to be their excellent natural best, to ensure that the workplaces they lead are places of joy where people enjoy and flourish in their work to be *their* natural best. Leading with moral courage, building authentic trust, and adopting a living legacy mindset all contribute to a culture of joy.

If we are privileged enough to be able to choose the work we do, the people we lead, and the places we live, then we have to consider the fact that our existence on this planet is fleeting, and life is just too short for joyless and purposeless work. As leaders we have a duty and a responsibility to ensure that we are doing all we can to inspire, motivate, and bring joy to the people we lead. Spread the Joy!

THE LEADERS BOOK

Concluding Thoughts

Moral courage, authentic trust and a living legacy mindset. These are the enduring qualities that excellent leaders - people worthy of our trust and followership - exude. Our intention in this book is neither to present an impossible ideal nor a checklist of traits to accumulate. Rather, we hope to have injected a keen sense of what constitutes goodness in leadership and how your own unique edges, character and experiences can be sources of excellence in the service of others.

No one is inspired by a person who's lukewarm - neither hot nor cold. Recall someone who's made a lasting impression on you; it's unlikely that you'll use language such as "was sort-of inspiring" or "was sometimes quite kind" or "made a few good decisions here and there." There is a risk with a book such as ours that the reader feels that applying the principles requires a diluting of all that makes them unique, a dulling of the senses and so much compromise as to lose their own sense of identity. That is not what we hope for you - please never become tepid.

Some of the most famous and arguably highly effective leaders demonstrate this reality. They are brilliant in some areas - rallying people to their cause, making courageous choices, challenging conventions, standing against threat, opening new opportunities for their people - but less adept in others. As I write this, I think of some of the leadership greats - Sir Winston Churchill, Martin Luther King Jr and Mother Teresa - you may have other people in mind. If assessed in each of the fifteen chapters that we have written, how would they score? Probably off-the-scale in some qualities and good in others, but not extremely high in all areas, all of the time. That would be, quite frankly, impossible.

What sets apart the great from the destructive is their ability to recognise what's needed in any given moment. They are self-aware and not self-centred. They are adept at applying themselves, bringing just the very insights and energy that are needed for a given situation. They enjoy involving others with different peak styles and skills in the pursuit of even better outcomes for employees, customers and communities. Leadership talent like this gets us very excited indeed.

The fifteen chapters in this book are therefore less about accumulating higher scores in all areas all at once. Our intention is to convey the three enduring qualities of good leaders, those who lead for the good of us all. Moral courage, authentic trust and a living legacy mindset each have a constant place in the leadership journey. Particular moments require different aspects to be emphasised, yet if you as a leader hold all three together throughout, you cannot fail to use your power and influence for good.

And we need good leaders more than ever.

As you reach the conclusion of this book, we keenly hope that there are two or three ideas that resonate very strongly with you. Even if it's only a single sentence that has leapt from the page, can we encourage you to act and to do so within a matter of hours. The accumulation of ideas is merely the beginning of change. Each of us is judged not by our intentions, but by our actions. The whole point of leadership is change. It is only in applying ourselves differently that change happens.

We're grateful for your willingness to lead and serve others and wish you every success.

Phil, Kareena and Nicole

THE LEADERS BOOK

Notes

Moral Courage

Foreword

- The Cardinal Virtues - prudence (wisdom), temperance (restraint or self-control), fortitude (courage) and justice (fairness).
- "Serve to Lead" is the motto of the Royal Military Academy Sandhurst.

Chapter 1: Decide with High Conviction

- Consumer Value Stores (CVS) an American Healthcare Company founded in 1963, cvshealth.com
- Dr Matthew Anderson, The Centre for Army Leadership, *The Role of Leaders in Building a Culture of Moral Courage*: The Proceedings of the Centre for Army Leadership's 2017 Conference, (Sandhurst: Centre for Army Leadership, 2018).

Chapter 2: Implement with Compassion

- Richard and Dave - For the purposes of this book, real names have not been used.
- Potential Project cited in Rasmus Hougaard and Jacqueline Carter, *Compassionate Leadership: How to do Hard Things in a Human Way*, (Boston Massachusetts: Harvard Business Review Press, 2022).

Chapter 3: Resist Immediate Gratification

- Bravado – Definition taken from the Cambridge Dictionary

Chapter 4: Do the Right Thing

- It was in 1982 that Johnson and Johnson went through the crisis of the Tylenol Tragedy where Tylenol capsules were tampered with and replaced with cyanide-laced capsules. jnj.co.uk

- RMS Titanic was a British passenger liner, described as 'unsinkable' before it set sail on its maiden voyage, but sank in the North Atlantic Ocean on 15 April 1912 after hitting an iceberg.

- Socrates (c.469 - 399 BCE) was a Greek philosopher who due to his great influence is credited as the founder of Western Philosophy. He was sentenced to death by the drinking of hemlock, because of his nonconformity, impiety and corruption of the youth.

Chapter 5: Embrace the Defining Moments

- Joseph Badaracco, Professor of Business Ethics at Harvard Business School, hbs.edu

- Kees van der Graaf's, toekomstvormers.nl

- Chesley Burnett 'Sully' Sullenberger an airline pilot who is known for landing in the Hudson River in 2009, after both engines failed due to a bird strike.

- Dr Nicola Brink, Director of Public Health, Guernsey, Channel Islands was interviewed especially for this book publication.

Authentic Trust

Chapter 6: Do not Hide!

- Brené Brown, "Clear is Kind. Unclear is Unkind," October 15, 2018, brenebrown.com
- Indira Gandhi – Source and date unknown

Chapter 7: Relate Well

- John Andrew Holmes – Source and date unknown
- John Maxwell, "Want Better Relationships? Be Relatable!", May 21, 2019, johnmaxwell.com

Chapter 8: Walk the Walk

- Immanuel Kant, *Groundwork of Metaphysics of Morals*, (J.F Hartknoch, Riga, 1785).

Chapter 9: Exercise Good Judgement

- Project Implicit, Harvard Implicit Association Test, Harvard University, 2011, implicit.harvard.edu
- CB Insights, "The Top 12 Reasons Startups Fail" Research Report, August 3, 2021, cbinsights.com
- Lewis Carroll, *Alice's Adventures in Wonderland,* (UK: Macmillan, 1865).
- "Jam tomorrow and jam yesterday, but never jam today." This is apparently a clever word play on the Latin word "iam", which is pronounced "jam" and means "at this time" but not in the present tense. It's, as Alice says to the Queen, confusing!

Chapter 11: Share Power

- Empowerment – Definition taken from Merriam-Webster Dictionary, 2023, merriam-webster.com

- British politician, historian, and writer Lord Acton in April 1887 summarised his thoughts in a letter to fellow scholar Mandell Creighton.

- "With great power comes great responsibility" appears in the film, *Spider-Man: No Way Home* (2021).

- Simon Sinek, *Start with Why: How Great Leaders Inspire Everyone to Take Action*, (London: Portfolio Penguin, 2011).

- Henry Ford – Source and date unknown

- Southwest Airlines, "Bluer Skies: The Great Southwest Uniform Refresh", 1994, southwest50.com

Living Legacy

Chapter 12: Prioritise Purpose

- Simon Sinek, *Start with Why: How Great Leaders Inspire Everyone to Take Action*, (London: Portfolio Penguin, 2011).

- Mihaly Csikszentmihalyi, *Finding Flow: The Psychology of Engagement With Everyday Life*, (New York: Basic Books, 1997).

- Kenne Fant, *Alfred Nobel: A Biography*, (New York: Arcade Publishing, 1993).

- Alfred's brother died in France from a heart attack and, apparently, one French newspaper misreported that it was Alfred who had died - The alleged obituary was quickly corrected, and the original cannot be found.

Chapter 13: Think Beyond the Horizon

- Meriwether Lewis and William Clark, The 'Corps of Discovery' expedition from the Mississippi River to the West Coast and back. May 1804 – September 1806.

- Field Marshal Edmund Henry Hynman Allenby, 1st Viscount, Senior British Army Officer – urged his officers to "think to the finish"

- Dan Gilbert, "The Psychology of your Future Self," Ted Talks 2014, youtube.com/ted

- Breyten BreytenBach, "Book Review: Why are writers always the last to know?", *New York Times*, (March 28, 1993) – referencing an African proverb: "He who travels alone travels fastest, but in the company of friends you go farther." This idea also has English language origins, referenced in Rudyard Kipling's poem "The Winners".

Chapter 14: Make Leaders not just Followers!

- Tom Peters – Source and date unknown
- Martin Luther King Jr, "Where do we go from here?", Annual Report Delivered at the 11th Convention of the Southern Christian Leadership Conference, (Atlanta, GA, August 16).
- Margaret Heffernan, "Three Problems of Power", December 11, 2020,
- m-heffernan.medium.com
- Brenè Brown, Facebook post by Brené Brown, June 13, 2013.

Chapter 15: Consider Whole-Community Impact

- Edward Norton Lorenz (1917-2008) was an American mathematician and meteorologist and founder of the modern chaos theory in the 1960s; a theory that is concerned with unpredictable courses of events where systems are sensitive to initial conditions. The concept of the butterfly effect, where small changes have great consequences is linked to this idea.
- 'The Horseshoe Nails' is found in James Baldwin, *Fifty Famous People: A Book of Short Stories,* (Charleston, Bibliobazaar, 2006).

- Neil Gaiman and Terry Pratchett, *Good Omens: The Nice and Accurate Prophecies of Agnes Nutter, Witch,* (London: Gollancz, 1990).

THE LEADERS BOOK

About the Authors

Leaders exists to encourage and challenge good workplace leadership. The type of leadership that fosters healthy, thriving environments for their people. Leaders who draw out the very best human qualities from their people - creativity, problem solving, making the world a better place. Our team comprises practitioners with real-life leadership experience in business, public sector, charity and church environments.

Phil Eyre, founder, previously headed a Wealth Management business in both executive and non-executive capacities. He has board level experience in various charities, local and national as well as leading a church for a period before establishing Leaders in 2017.

Kareena Hodgson has spent over twenty years in leading and managing roles for a large national charity, including establishing and heading up their Guernsey services. She has experience representing the voluntary sector at multi-agency board level and on various committees.

Nicole Le Goupillot was previously a teacher of Philosophy, Ethics and Religion and senior leader at an Elim Pentecostal Church, having achieved degrees in Child, Family and Educational Studies as well as Theology. She is an ordained Reverend and an appointed RAF Air Cadet Chaplain.

Our work brings insight, clarity, guidance and accountability to individual leaders and leadership teams across a wide spectrum of business sectors, charities and public services. Our forte is in facilitating conversations that illuminate the critical issues, whether in a coaching, leadership group or team offsite setting. We're frequently invited to speak at leadership events.

THE LEADERS BOOK

THE LEADERS BOOK

About PublishU

PublishU is transforming the world of publishing.

PublishU has developed a new and unique approach to publishing books, offering a three-step guided journey to becoming a globally published author!

We enable hundreds of people a year to write their book within 100-days, publish their book in 100-days and launch their book over 100-days to impact tens of thousands of people worldwide.

The journey is transformative, one author said,

"I never thought I would be able to write a book, let alone in 100 days... now I'm asking myself what else have I told myself that can't be done that actually can?'"

To find out more visit
www.PublishU.com

Printed in Great Britain
by Amazon